Between Persecution and Participation

Modern Jewish History
Henry Feingold, *Series Editor*

Select Titles in Modern Jewish History

Between Persecution and Participation

Biography of a Bookkeeper at J. A. Topf & Söhne

Annegret Schüle
and **Tobias Sowade**

Translated from the German by
Penny Milbouer

With a Foreword by
Michael Thad Allen

Syracuse University Press

Originally published in German as *Willy Wiemokli: Buchhalter bei J. A. Topf & Söhne—zwischen Verfolgung und Mitwisserschaft* (Berlin: Hentrich & Hentrich Verlag, 2015).

∞ The paper used in this publication meets the minimum requirements of the American National Standard for Information Sciences—Permanence of Paper for Printed Library Materials, ANSI Z39.48-1992.

For a listing of books published and distributed by Syracuse University Press, visit www.SyracuseUniversityPress.syr.edu.

ISBN: 978-0-8156-3610-6 (hardcover)
   978-0-8156-3616-8 (paperback)
   978-0-8156-5463-6 (e-book)

Library of Congress Cataloging-in-Publication Data

Names: Schüle, Annegret, 1959– author. | Sowade, Tobias, 1988– author. | Milbouer, Penny, translator.

Title: Between persecution and participation : biography of a bookkeeper at J. A. Topf & Söhne / Annegret Schüle and Tobias Sowade ; translated from the German by Penny Milbouer.

Other titles: Willy Wiemokli. English

Description: Syracuse, New York : Syracuse University Press, [2018] | Series: Modern Jewish history | Includes bibliographical references.

Identifiers: LCCN 2018035341 (print) | LCCN 2018036155 (ebook) | ISBN 9780815654636 (E-book) | ISBN 9780815636106 (hardcover : alk. paper) | ISBN 9780815636168 (pbk. : alk. paper)

Subjects: LCSH: Wiemokli, Willy, 1908–1983. | Firma J.A. Topf & Söhne—Employees. | Accountants—Germany—Biography. | Mischlinge (Nuremberg Laws of 1935)—Germany—Biography. | Holocaust, Jewish (1939–1945)

Classification: LCC DS134.42.W534 (ebook) | LCC DS134.42.W534 S3813 2018 (print) | DDC 940.53/18092 [B] —dc23

LC record available at https://lccn.loc.gov/2018035341

Manufactured in Canada

Vergangenes historisch artikulieren heisst nicht, es erkennen "wie es denn eigentlich gewesen ist." Es heisst, sich einer Erinnerung bemächtigen, wie sie im Augenblick einer Gefahr aufblitzt.

—Walter Benjamin, *Über den Begriff der Geschichte*

To articulate what the past historically is does not mean to recognize "how it really was." It means to seize control of a memory, as it flares up in a moment of danger.

Contents

Illustrations and Table

Illustrations

ix

Table

Foreword

Michael Thad Allen

Willy Wiemokli, a half Jew under the Nuremberg Laws, worked in the accounting department at Topf & Söhne, the company that engineered the crematoria ovens and the gas chamber ventilation system used in Auschwitz. Topf & Söhne was one of the many companies, large and small, that furnished goods and services to the Nazi regime, which ranged from banal items to the wares of murder.

These companies dealt with the special division of the SS called the Wirtschaftsverwaltungshauptamt (Business Administration Main Office) or WVHA, which oversaw the Zentralbauleitung der Waffen-SS und Polizei Auschwitz (Central Construction Headquarters of the Waffen-SS and Auschwitz Police) or ZBL. The engineers of Topf & Söhne dealt directly and in person with ZBL personnel, such as its chief engineer, Karl Bischoff. He was admired for his organizational talent,

Parts of this essay formed a part of *The Business of Genocide: The SS, Slave Labor, and the Concentration Camps* (Chapel Hill: Univ. of North Carolina Press, 2002). Used by permission.

which included increasing the scale and scope of what might be called a genocide-industrial complex at Auschwitz-Birkenau. Unfortunately, we know little about Bischoff or his motivations, but his SS staff included one officer who intermarried with a Polish woman, something that did not seem to concern him. But there is also no evidence that he had compunctions about the business of genocide.

The WVHA organized the business of genocide while Willy Wiemokli found refuge at its contractor, Topf & Söhne. This cruel paradox invites a comparison between Topf & Söhne, still in many respects a traditional, paternalistic firm. This is not to say that it was stuck in medieval guild customs, yet Topf & Söhne had passed from father to son; its owners still exerted themselves both to know their workers personally and to run operations directly; they also prided themselves on customizing products for their clients. The WVHA, by comparison, tried (not always successfully) to embody modern, impersonal management and mass production new to the early twentieth century.

Comparisons, however, should avoid false dichotomies. Topf & Söhne, founded in 1878, had become a global leader in its industry under the leadership of the next generation by the 1900s. Every oven Topf & Söhne delivered to the SS was designed to specifications, installed, tested, and repaired on-site. The SS acquired them under the usual forms for purchase orders and invoices. Personnel under Topf & Söhne's chief engineer, Kurt Prüfer, were regularly called upon to troubleshoot the system alongside SS engineers—as any vendor would be. The commercial enterprise of genocide was unusual and horrific, but in this mundane sense it was not different from business conducted among firms then or now. However, neither the WVHA nor Topf & Söhne personnel were mindless automatons ensnared in an ideological machine. They were, of course, motivated by managerial pride, a desire for engineering prowess, loyalty to their group, and nationalism. How Willy Wiemokli understood his role in this process—a process that would ultimately lead to the industrial murder of his father—is harder to perceive, not least because he left no record of it. He also had the powerful need to support and protect himself and his parents when no one else would give him a job.

Wiemokli found refuge within the paternalistic employment of Topf & Söhne—a very different world from big corporations like Siemens or the new National Socialist automobile manufacturer, Volkswagen. Topf & Söhne began as a family enterprise, born of an entrepreneurial and engineering founder, Johannes Andreas Topf, during the great German economic expansion of the late nineteenth century known as the *Gründerzeit*. Germany established itself (with the United States) as a first mover in the second industrial revolution—a revolution of electrical power, synthetic organic chemicals, and modern manufacturing. Then, as now, there were many more innovative small or medium-sized businesses like Topf & Söhne than there were giant corporations. As a whole, however, large and small companies, dynamic research universities, and government-funded research institutes formed an industrial ecosystem that maintained an explosion of technical and scientific knowledge and its swift application in useful industries.

By the 1930s, Topf & Söhne was in the hands of the third generation, Ernst Wolfgang and Ludwig Topf. By that time, the company had long been preeminent in its sector, principally manufacturing of heat-transfer technology and automation for the brewery industry, with the manufacture of crematoria as a marginal side business. Topf & Söhne prided itself on maintaining its competitive advantage at the forefront of technological change. It combined this with the management of a skilled workforce that could customize production according to the needs of individual customers. The firm's corporate values included a paternalistic commitment and loyalty to Topf employees, which they also appear to have reciprocated—including Wiemokli, who consistently defended Ernst Wolfgang Topf and his family after the war. Ernst Wolfgang Topf had also intervened for Willy Wiemokli when the Gestapo brought him in for questioning about possible *Rassenschande* (consorting with an Aryan woman). In the setting of a small, paternalistic enterprise, the company's loyalty was personal, not abstract, and it was easily compatible with using slave labor or marketing products for the Nazi genocide—which befell outsiders.

The contrast to its customer, the SS, is instructive. The WVHA's key personnel prided themselves on being modern men, who wished to remake Europe in the name of a millenarian Nazi vision of modern society. They had usually received systematic training in some aspect of modern administration or other modern professions—business management, for example—rather than abstract economics. Many also had higher degrees in business law, civil engineering, or architecture.

By training, Wiemokli himself belonged to this rising managerial, or white-collar, class in retail and office work. Wiemokli dated a German gentile, Erika Glass, whom he could marry only after the war. Willy Wiemokli worked in the modern commercial sector, as did Erika, and, unusual for women at that time, Erika had a managerial position. In another time and place this would have been a "modern" family on the rise, leaning in with ambition, education, and skill to escape provincial boundaries. Even in Germany in the 1930s, lacking a stable democratic society, under the rule of National Socialism, their aspirations in a rapidly modernizing society—but cut short for Willy Wiemokli by the Nuremberg Laws and literally reflected by the changes in his occupation listed in the city address book—were not so very different from the WVHA's managers. The difference is that they had little power or agency—the WVHA's managers did.

Nevertheless, the Third Reich mobilized the new managerial class. These men took pride in their organizational skills, and National Socialism seduced many of them with its ideology of national renewal. During the Weimar Republic, for instance, the political right succeeded in mobilizing the activism of Germany's elite engineering students. Taught that their profession was rational and the engine of industrial growth, engineering students believed their technical skills were the means to bring about the betterment of mankind and of their nation. But the turmoil of the Weimar Republic all but insured that their ambitions bore rotted fruit. Free markets and democracy were in turmoil—not only in Germany but throughout the West. Industry was wrecked. Innovations such as Fordism were on the rise, but economic dislocation frustrated the spread of new technology and organization in industry and business.

The men attracted to serve in the WVHA typically rose from this milieu. They were also set off from the leadership corps of the concentration camps, the *Kommandanten*, who usually had little education and excelled only at terror and brutality. Reichsführer-SS Heinrich Himmler eventually directed the WVHA to take over the concentration camps in an effort to modernize and industrialize them. Indeed, the push for slave labor, especially before 1942, was driven by the need perceived by Himmler to make the camps a vital link in the industrial supply chain for German settlements he intended to build throughout the conquered territories of Eastern Europe.

Himmler's "New Order for Europe" required coordination of industry on a huge scale, which necessitated the expansion of the concentration camps, the organization of building materials and transport, as well as the reorganization of prisoner management. The camps were not, at first, part of the country's military operations, producing weapons or military supplies. (Later, after 1942, the camps expanded yet again to provide slave labor for some of Germany's most advanced weapons projects, like the V-2 rockets.) The SS first converted an old, abandoned powder factory at Dachau into a prison camp in 1933, and eventually more and more camps were built before the war. Then, with Germany's invasion and occupation of Poland in 1939, still more camps were added, beginning with Auschwitz in 1940. This required administrative and engineering skills—and the SS rallied its administrators by appealing to their ideological esprit de corps—which could vary from Nazi fundamentalism to pride in working together to accomplishing difficult and complex projects.

For the WVHA, this meant reorganizing SS-owned industries and internal departments. The SS chose as its business model the interlocking hierarchy of the large vertically integrated, modern corporation. The SS preferred mass production and large-scale centralized organizations to the kind of smaller scale and customized production typical of Topf &

Söhne. The SS looked for modern methods and technological innovations, but also overlooked the ways in which smaller firms thrived through innovation and swift adaptation.

Thus, it was no accident that when the WVHA needed customized supplies, such as the crematoria for Auschwitz, they did not manufacture these in-house. Rather, the SS sought out a world-class manufacturer and industry leader like Topf & Söhne, which was not a mass-production manufacturer but produced the tools of mass production to other industries. It was also typical of the synergy between large-scale, modern industry and small and medium-sized businesses like Topf & Söhne that the latter, a family owned business, sold its products all over Germany, Europe, and as far away as the United States, Russia, Japan, and South America.

The WVHA was too large for most mid- or lower-level managers to know each other personally—unlike a family firm like Topf & Söhne. Rather than personal loyalty, the glue that held the WVHA together was shared commitment to a common cause. And where managers' values differed, this could also tear the organization apart. Within the WVHA, conflicts arose over the multiplicity of meanings within Nazi ideology. Differences could lead to turmoil and failure even among competent managers. Some had promoted National Socialism from their youth; others only sympathized but could not be called fanatics. The SS was the radical vanguard of a radical political movement (National Socialism), and members of the WVHA were certainly conscious of the aims of the organization they worked for. They were not cogs in a machine. As a rule, they had authority and were conscious of their command and control.

SS-Gruppenführer Oswald Pohl, whom Reichsführer Himmler placed at the head of the WVHA, was a Nazi fundamentalist already in the 1920s, and made a name for himself by modernizing the administrative structure of the German navy. He had also briefly studied law, joining the Nazi Party in 1926, where he became a confidant of Himmler (who was ten years his junior). As head of the WVHA, he was one of the most powerful men in the SS, although he remains lesser known than Reinhardt Heydrich or even Theodor Eicke, whom he supplanted as head of the concentration camp's industrial empire. In addition to converting the camps into an industrial base for the SS's fantasy projects for the realization of racial supremacy, he also worked with Albert Speer and others to broker slave labor across Europe.

As he had modernized the German navy, Pohl and the men he recruited to the top and middle ranks of the WVHA also modernized the management of the SS. Whereas traditional bureaucracies relied on prestige of a high rank in state service, which clothed bureaucrats in the authority and power of the sovereign, the new professions claimed authority based on their knowledge and efficiency. The WVHA strove to adopt the new managerial techniques of modern industry. This also meant demonstrating success in terms of yield, time, and profit rather than simple methodical record keeping or promotion within the ranks of state service. Modern bureaucracies use numbers to record and chronicle information, which they tailored to command and control operations. The model for modern bureaucracy never was the traditional European civil service but the modern, American corporation new to the late nineteenth and early twentieth centuries' most dynamic corporations (e.g., Siemens or AEG in Germany; DuPont or

General Electric in the United States). German managers had been fascinated by the American efficiency movement well before 1933.

Pohl's WVHA imposed these new methods on the concentration camps. For example, under the leadership of Pohl's top manager of the camp industries, Gerhard Maurer, Pohl replaced prose reports with statistical reporting for the quick communication of information needed to manage slave labor. A grim example is the evolution of the registers of the dead known as the "Death Books" of Auschwitz. Originally kept as bound ledgers, these typically chronicled information such as the date of death, name, and prisoner number, as well as the deceased's place of origin, although the SS was obviously trying to erase these people. The "Death Books" also recorded the names of the father and mother of the deceased. This information had no conceivable relationship to the industries or the operations in which these prisoners worked. The purpose was descriptive rather than command and control. Those in command positions generally made scant reference to the "Death Books," which differed little from similar (although obviously different) records kept by medieval churches recording parish deaths, marriages, and baptisms. It was usually the state, not managers of industry, that cherished this kind of detailed information, the embodiment of Europe's 1,500-year-old tradition of bureaucracy.

The "Death Books" were of little use to the WVHA's management of slave labor. As German airframe manufacture, V-2 rocket production, and other breakneck war projects began placing ever larger requests for concentration camp prisoners, the SS ceased recording the extraneous information in the "Death Books" in 1943. Gerhard Maurer still required the data, but the WVHA stripped out prisoners' names, place of origin, and parents' names—depersonalizing the textured history of the fit and the dead. Instead, Maurer ordered prison doctors to keep aggregate statistics that parsed prison populations into the "fit" and "unfit" to work. This accelerated the speed with which the SS could gather information and sufficed to ship requisitioned prisoners to factories throughout Germany. Maurer did so by distributing standardized forms for the prison doctors to fill out, which his office collected regularly. Collated in graphs and charts, this enabled Maurer to monitor mortality rates at a glance. With this information at their fingertips, the WVHA's managers could react quickly to fluctuations and spot disruptions to the flow of prisoners, such as typhus outbreaks.

Maurer's rationalization met with some resistance among the *Kommandanten*, whose training and motivations differed markedly from that of the industrial managers whom Pohl struggled throughout the war to set over them. Maurer succeeded enough, however, so that information flowed more quickly, and made possible the centralized command and control over slave labor for the first time. He was also typical of the ambitious professional men of the 1920s and 1930s who, like the activist Pohl, ascended to the top ranks of the WVHA.

Inasmuch as Willy Wiemokli's life expressed a loyal work ethic, he had much in common with the SS men who murdered his father and managed camp industry. He too had acquired modern business skills, which he used after the war to rescue Topf & Söhne from Soviet mismanagement. He also did his best to shield the company and its owners from the Soviets. In other words, Willy Wiemokli is a figure of continuity into the postwar period, working to retain the ethos of the small family owned enterprise even when Topf & Söhne became a state-owned enterprise.

The WVHA's top managers did not invent National Socialist ideology or the practices of modern management and production. They only strove to adapt and apply them. Their belief that their skills and methods embodied the prowess of the German race in commerce and technology—including administering death and misery on an industrial scale—demonstrates how modernization can also be married to the most irrational and extreme ideologies. At least before the end of National Socialism in 1945, they saw themselves as men on the rise.

By contrast, Willy Wiemokli's life was acid-washed by multiple criminal regimes and etched by one cruel tragedy after another. The constant in his personal and working life was reciprocated personal loyalty, which he showed to Ernst Wolfgang Topf; his wife, Erika Glass; colleagues; and neighbors. Annegret Schüle's and Tobias Sowade's biography of Willy Wiemokli examines a life that is significant for its place in the larger historical context, but certainly remarkable on its own terms: as for so many of that period, Willy Wiemokli's main achievement in his life turns out to have been survival with his personal relationships intact—no small feat.

Acknowledgments

This book stands alone and at the same time adds to the research of the corporate history of Topf & Söhne by Annegret Schüle (www.topfundsoehne.de).

We thank Jutta Hoschek, Christiane Kuller, Harry Stein, and Sabine Stein for their assistance in research. We also thank Frank Boblenz and Erinnerungsort Topf & Söhne (Topf & Söhne—Builders of the Ovens of Auschwitz Place of Remembrance) for their assistance with archival material and the copyrights for the images. We also thank Verena Bunkus, Sophie Eckenstaler, and Susann Haase for copyediting the manuscript.

—Annegret Schüle and Tobias Sowade

I thank Hentrich & Hentrich Verlag in Berlin, whose extraordinary program of books on Jewish history and personalities includes *Willy Wiemokli: Buchhalter bei J. A. Topf & Söhne—zwischen Verfolgung und Mitwisserschaft*. I am grateful for Annegret Schüle's patient and careful review and her helpful suggestions. I am also grateful to the anonymous readers and to the editors at Syracuse University Press.

—Penny Milbouer

Abbreviations

APMO — Archiv des Staatlichen Museums Auschwitz-Birkenau (Archive of the State Museum of Auschwitz-Birkenau)

HHStAW — Hessisches Hauptstaatsarchiv Wiesbaden (Hessian Main State Archive Wiesbaden)

ITS — International Tracing Service, Digital Archive, Bad Arolsen

StadtA Erfurt — Stadtarchiv Erfurt (Erfurt City Archive)

LaTh–HStAW — Landesarchiv Thüringen–Hauptstaatsarchiv Weimar (State Archive of Thuringia–Main State Archive Weimar)

LaTh–StAG — Landesarchiv Thüringen–Staatsarchiv Gotha (State Archive of Thuringia–State Archive Gotha)

Between Persecution
and Participation

Family and Youth

Willi Hermann Wyjmoklyj was born on December 5, 1908, in Halle (Saale), Germany.[1] His father, David, was thirty-two years old; his mother, Anna (née Kaufmann), was ten years younger. Willi would be the couple's only child. The day after he was born his father was baptized in Leipzig as a Protestant. On New Year's Eve 1908, a Thursday, the young parents married in the registry office of Halle-North;[2] they were then wed in a church ceremony by a Protestant clergyman.[3] The three-week-old Willi might have been baptized in the same service. He was definitely baptized as a Protestant. Little is known about his mother, Anna Kaufmann. She was born in Aschersleben, about fifty kilometers northwest of Halle, on January 14, 1886, and came from a Protestant family.[4]

We know a little more about Willi's father. The salesman David Wyjmoklyj was born in Berlin on October 13, 1876, to a Jewish family that included his two sisters, Sara and Pauline; his mother, Esther (née Wischnewitz); and his father, Nachmann Lejb Wyjmoklyj. Nachmann sold shoes at Weisestrasse 16 in the Berlin district of Neukölln.[5] Nachmann and Esther, Willi's paternal grandparents, were Polish Jews. Nachmann Wyjmoklyj, who was born in 1852, came from Meseritz in the province of Lublin.[6] Meseritz (today Międzyrec Podlaski),

1

165 kilometers east of Warsaw, was one of those East Polish shtetls, characterized by a high proportion of Jewish inhabitants, which completely lost its identity with the destruction of Polish Jewry during the Holocaust. Willi's grandmother Esther probably came from Łuków, about thirty kilometers from Meseritz, which in 1851, the year she was born, belonged to the Kingdom of Poland controlled by Russia, as was her husband's native city.[7] Nachmann and Esther Wyjmoklyj came to Berlin at the beginning of the 1870s and thus were part of the large group of Ostjuden (Eastern European Jews) who were fleeing disfranchisement, poverty, lack of opportunity, and a heightened fear of pogroms under Russian rule. The young couple probably hoped for a better future in Berlin after the German Empire, founded in 1871, granted equal civil rights to all religious confessions for the first time throughout the empire.

The date of death for Esther Wyjmoklyj is undocumented. Nachmann Wyjmoklyj died when Willi was fifteen years old, and thus it may be that Willi at least came in touch with the rich, centuries-old culture of Polish Jews through his grandfather.[8] Why David Wyjmoklyj decided to convert to Protestantism the day after his son's birth is unknown. On the one hand, the civil emancipation of German Jews had introduced a good period in German-Jewish relations. On the other hand—in reaction to this success and the accomplishments of Jews in Germany—anti-Semitism that Christianity had shaped for centuries now became an anti-Semitism shaped by racist arguments, which had a significant impact on the daily life of many Jews and on opportunities available for success. David Wyjmoklyj's baptism could well have been the effort to protect his marriage and his infant son from anti-Semitic

1. Excerpt from the *Ahnentafel* (genealogical table) for David Wyj-moklyj. It is from the files of the Magistrate's Court of Erfurt, which concerns a penalty order against him dated February 15, 1943. Original: LA-Thüringen-Staatsarchiv Gotha, Amtsgericht Erfurt (Magistrate's Court Erfurt) no. 1006, leaf 5.

hostility. Furthermore, even though he himself had been born in Berlin, there was the fact that he lacked German citizenship because of his parents' origins. In light of his precarious status as a foreigner, perhaps he wanted at least to shed the stigma of being Jewish. David Wyjmoklyj's baptism, as well as his marriage to Anna after Willi was born, unambiguously signaled a choice of direction: the Wyjmoklyjs had now become a Protestant family.

In May 1921 the married couple and twelve-year-old Willi moved from Halle to Erfurt. The family lived at first at Neuwerkstrasse 28 for a few weeks, then at Scharnhorststrasse 8 (today Stauffenbergallee), and finally after October 1921 they lived in the southwestern part of Erfurt at Gustav-Adolf-Strasse

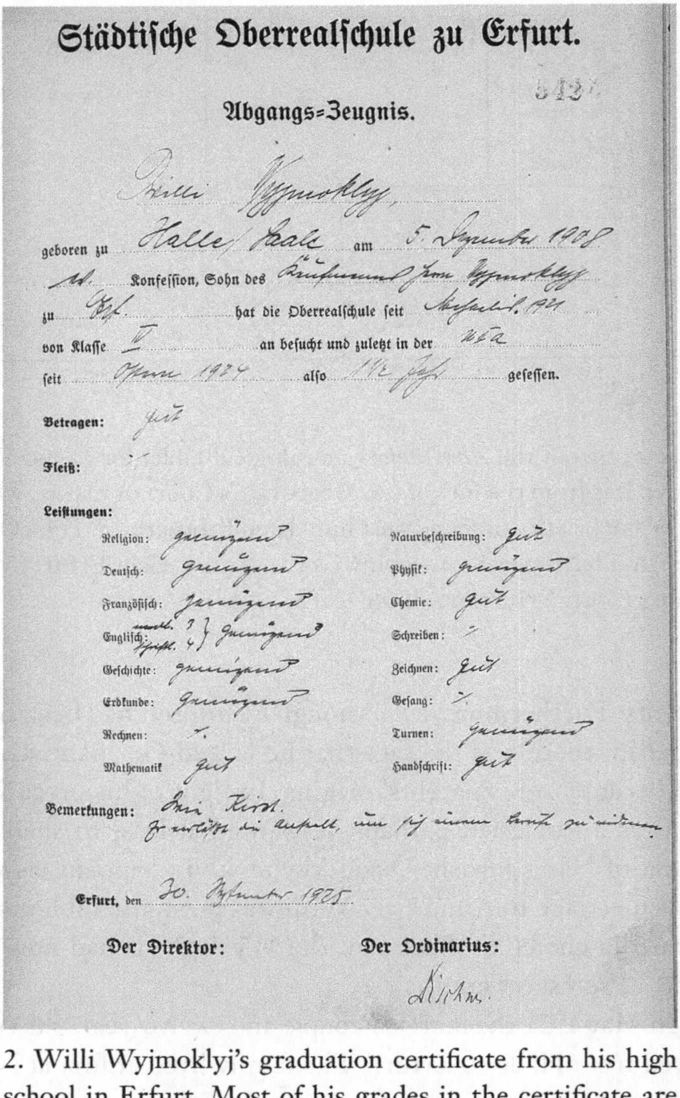

Städtische Oberrealschule zu Erfurt.

Abgangs=Zeugnis.

Willi Wyjmoklyj,

geboren zu Halle/Saale am 5. Dezember 1908

ev. Konfession, Sohn des Kaufmanns Iwan Wyjmoklyj

zu Erf. hat die Oberrealschule seit Michaelis 1921

von Klasse VI an besucht und zuletzt in der U II a

seit Ostern 1924 also 1 1/2 Jahr gesessen.

Betragen: gut

Fleiß: –

Leistungen:

Religion:	genügend	Naturbeschreibung:	gut
Deutsch:	genügend	Physik:	genügend
Französisch:	genügend	Chemie:	gut
Englisch: mündl. 3, schriftl. 4	genügend	Schreiben:	–
Geschichte:	genügend	Zeichnen:	gut
Erdkunde:	genügend	Gesang:	–
Rechnen:	–	Turnen:	genügend
Mathematik	gut	Handschrift:	gut

Bemerkungen: Frei Kirch.
Er verläßt die Anstalt, um sich einem Berufe zu widmen.

Erfurt, den 30. September 1925

Der Direktor: **Der Ordinarius:**

Kirchn.

2. Willi Wyjmoklyj's graduation certificate from his high school in Erfurt. Most of his grades in the certificate are "satisfactory," but in mathematics he received the grade of "good," a useful credential for a future salesman. StadtA Erfurt 1-2/232-4244, leaf 542.

2a in a fourth-floor apartment.[9] The three were to live together for over thirty years, until Willi's parents died in 1942 and 1943. In the address book of the city of Erfurt for 1922–23, David Wyjmoklyj is mentioned for the first time with his profession listed as *Kaufmann* (salesman) (see table, p. 8).[10] In the autumn of 1921, Willi entered the public secondary school in Erfurt.[11] The modern school building at Krämpferring 25 (today Juri-Gagarin-Ring 126) had opened its doors in 1909. The school boasted excellent facilities: an observatory, workshops (metal-working, blacksmithing, carpentry), a gymnasium, a library, and an auditorium with a grand piano and an organ enriched the pupils' daily routine.[12]

On September 30, 1925, Willi Wyjmoklyj graduated with an *Obersekundarreife*, the tenth-grade graduation certificate. In choosing his career, Willi apparently followed his father and grandfather. Both were involved in the shoe trade, and he too stayed in the clothing retail business. Immediately after finishing school, Willi Wyjmoklyj began training to become a retail employee in the Erfurt department store Römischer Kaiser, and after his apprenticeship he had a number of positions in various places.[13]

From Wyjmoklyj to Wiemokli (and Back)

Although Willi Wyjmoklyj still bore the name of his Polish forebears on his graduation certificate in 1925, starting in 1924 his father was listed for the first time in the address book of the city of Erfurt as David Wiemokli, footwear and shoe salesman (see table, p. 8). His name on his file card in Erfurt's civil register is spelled this way, probably amended in 1938 with the remark "see also Wyjmoklyj/see foreigner card file, family page placed here, children are *Mischlinge* (mixed race)."[1] In November 1938, as inmates in the KZ (*Konzentrationslager*, concentration camp) of Buchenwald, father and son were listed as Wyjmoklyj, but the only name was Willy Wiemokli, who in 1939 started working at J. A. Topf & Söhne, with the *y* from the family name gone, reappearing in the first name of Willy. When David was sentenced to a month's imprisonment in 1943 and then deported to Auschwitz, where he was murdered, police, court files, and the death certificate list the name as David Israel Wyjmoklyj. In the address book of the city of Erfurt for 1948, there is a Willy Wyjmoklyj listed as a department manager, and in 1950 there is a Willi Wiemokli with the same description. The District Court for Erfurt, which sentenced

6

him to three years in prison on November 18, 1953, turned the man who had been calling himself almost all along Willy Wiemokli into the defendant Willy Wyjmoklyj. His identity card as a Persecuted Person of the Nazi Regime (VdN) is issued to Willi Wiemokli; the memorial in the grove of honor for those the German Democratic Republic (GDR) honored as a VdN bears the name Willy Wyjmoklyj in Erfurt's main cemetery to this day. In these frequent name shifts one can see a connection, even if it isn't free of contradictions. When David Wyjmoklyj first came to Erfurt he probably saw that his Polish-sounding name hurt his career, so he Germanized the name. When his son entered the work force, he followed the same strategy of adaptation. The Weimar Republic was liberal with respect to names, allowing a change with justification from a foreign name to a German one. Under National Socialism the possibility of Germanizing one's name was basically abolished—it was, after all, a question of protecting the *deutsche Blut-und Volksgemeinschaft* (German blood and folk community) from people of an "inferior race." Even if the Wiemoklis had registered their change of name lawfully in the 1920s, and we don't know this, the original name apparently was now discovered in the documents by eager bureaucrats in registry offices and courts and, probably against the will of the man who bore the name, was reactivated. That the authorities of the German Democratic Republic followed the National Socialist practice is striking. The use of both versions of the name in different sources of similar date every now and then presents the authors of this book with some problems. We have tried to use the version that was used in the relevant historical context, but in the case of doubt we chose the name that the person in question had chosen himself to the extent that this could be ascertained.

Versions of Wyjmoklyj/Wiemokli in Address Books of Erfurt

Year (vol. no.)	Closing Date	Name and occupation indicated in the alphabetical directory. Gustav-Adolf-Strasse 2a III is the address throughout
1921 (no vol. no. given)	December 1920	. . .
1922–1923 (no vol. no. given)	March 1922	Wyjmoklyj, David, salesman
1924 (no vol. no. given)	June	Wiemokli, David, footwear representative
1926 (no vol. no. given)	July	Wiemokli, David, footwear representative
1928 (71)	January	Wiemokli, David, footwear representative
1930 (72)	January	Wiemokli, David, footwear representative
1931–1932 (73)	November 1931	Wiemokli, David, salesman Wiemokli, Willy, salesman
1933 (74)	September	Wiemokli, David, salesman Wiemokli, Willy, salesman
1935 (75)	End of June	Wiemokli, David, salesman Wiemokli, Willy, salesman
1936 (76)	No date given	Wiemokli, David, salesman, P Erf 26819 Wiemokli, Willy, salesman
1937–1938 (77)	September 1937	Wiemokli, David, salesman Wiemokli, Willy, shop assistant
1938 (78)	October	Wiemokli, Willy, clerk
1939–1940 (79)	November 1939	Wiemokli, Willy, clerk
1941–1942 (80)	July 1941	Wiemokli, Willy, clerk
1948 (81)	Beginning of 1948	Wyjmoklyj, Willy, department manager
1950 (82)	July	Wiemokli, Willi, department head T 7313

Source: Address books of the city of Erfurt.

After October 1938 there is no further mention of David Wiemokli. The address books are consecutive. They were prepared from the civil registries and from information researched by the publisher of the address books. The last address book in the GDR was published in 1950, after which date there were only official telephone books.

Apprenticeship in the Department Store Römischer Kaiser

Is it by chance that Willi Wyjmoklyj, a Protestant with Jewish roots, completed his apprenticeship at the department store Römischer Kaiser? Opened in 1908, where the same impressive Jugendstil building still houses the department store Anger 1 (Karstadt) today, this enormously successful department store belonged to Jews. After the houses at the addresses of Anger 1–3 in Erfurt, including the Hotel Römischer Kaiser, were destroyed by fire in 1905, Hermann Tietz and his nephews Oscar and Leonhard Tietz purchased the land in 1906 through their Berlin land-acquisition company, and together with Siegfried Pinthus and Arthur Arndtheim of Erfurt they financed the construction of the department store.[1] It became the largest and most successful department store in Thuringia and it attracted visitors from far beyond the city borders.

The glass sphere on the roof measured four meters in diameter, and at dusk it was illuminated from within. The new owner removed this international landmark of the Jewish founders immediately after Aryanization in 1937.

Elderly Erfurt women can still recall how the modern elevator, the great array of goods for sale from all over the world,

3. The department store Römischer Kaiser in the 1920s. StadtA Erfurt, 6-0/86.

and the lavish illumination of the façade had impressed them as children. Siegfried Pinthus (1870–1937) and the brother of his wife, Hedwig (1882–1942), Arthur Arndtheim (1879–1945) were the owners and managing directors. Arthur's and Hedwig's mother, Cassandra, was born into the prominent Tietz family that had become famous for building department store empires. At the beginning of the twentieth century, the brothers Leonhard (1849–1914) and Oscar Tietz (1858–1923), who had started out with small businesses in Stralsund and Gera, already had a number of department stores throughout the Wilhelmine German Empire. After 1926, KaDeWe (Kaufhaus des Westens), which had opened in Berlin nineteen years earlier, also joined the empire of their offspring. Today it is the largest department store on the European continent, with approximately sixty thousand square meters of sales space.[2]

Like many other important businessmen of Erfurt, Arndtheim and Pinthus were active in the Jewish community, which in 1925 had 935 members and by 1932 had increased to 1,290.[3] In 1927 Pinthus was one of the founders of the Association for Jewish History and Literature, and in 1933 he was the chairman of the Jewish community. His wife, Hedwig, was active as the chair of the Israelite Women's Association. Arndtheim also held important positions in the community. He was the secretary of their most important committee, the Representative Assembly, and member of the Cultural Affairs Committee. It is safe to say that the number of Jewish men and women who worked at the Römischer Kaiser was above average. Even though the personnel files for the period from 1908 to 1948 for a total of eight thousand employees are now impossible to find, it is known, for example, that some employees gave notice after 1933 because they were emigrating to Palestine, South Africa, or Argentina—a clear sign they were persecuted because they were Jewish.[4]

Willi Wyjmoklyj won the lottery when he got an apprenticeship to become a salesman in the Römischer Kaiser department store beginning in the autumn of 1925. The apprenticeship training there enjoyed a good reputation.[5] Nonetheless, during his three-year apprenticeship he saw the hostility directed at his employer and the store itself. The middle of the nineteenth century in France saw the development of department store principles, which offered fixed prices, no pressure to buy, and allowed the customer to exchange the purchase. These developments revolutionized the shopping culture and were brought by Jewish businessmen to Germany with great success. Inspired by the department store pioneers Tietz, the Römischer Kaiser also offered a diverse assortment across a wide range of goods, low prices, good quality with high turnover, buying wholesale from producers as well as special sales and innovative forms of advertising. When an east-facing addition opened on November 17, 1927, the sales area almost doubled. Up to thirty thousand customers a day for special events was proof of the improvement in quality and increase in popularity. Even during the construction of the addition on the rear of the building the directors planned to redesign the façades and, most importantly, to increase the number of floors from four to seven. They had the building permit in hand.

Just then, in December 1925, the anti-Semitic and anti-democratic Erfurt weekly *Echo Germania* made the Römischer Kaiser the focus of its smear campaigns. The editor, Adolf Schmalix (b. 1890, in Oberpfalz [Upper Palatinate, in eastern Bavaria]), had been active in the *Rätebewegung* (workers' council movement) for a short while in Kiel in 1918 and had participated in the Hitler putsch in 1923, resulting in a prison term. In 1924 he moved to Erfurt. Although he had a long criminal record as a sex offender and used his newspaper as blackmail, Schmalix's demagoguery gained him a large political influence.[6] In 1927 Schmalix wrote in an article titled "Department Store Fever" that the "Hebrew consumer temple," "southern voracity," and "Jewish business practices" would drive the "Erfurt business community" into poverty.[7] He exploited the anxieties of small shop owners and tradespeople, who feared for their existence in the face of the inexorable modernization of consumer habits brought about by the rise of the department store culture, and Schmalix pushed these fears in the direction of racism and anti-Semitism. He preached getting rid of Jews from the economy and society as the cure for economic and social misery. He called Siegfried Pinthus and the department store Römischer Kaiser "the scourge of society among the business community and tradespeople in Erfurt."[8] Schmalix actually was successful with his hate campaign in blocking the increase in size of the department store.[9] Just how widespread anti-Semitism was in Erfurt can be seen in the Grossdeutscher Freiheitsbewegung (Greater German Freedom Movement), founded by Schmalix in 1928. At the end of 1929 it received the most votes in the city elections, and with ten out of fifty-two seats it became the strongest faction in the city parliament next to the Social Democrats (SPD). This election result embarrassed the city in the eyes of the liberals throughout the Weimar Republic. The *Münchner Zeitung* mocked, "Erfurt, Erfurt—we fear your honor is done for with this man."* And the *Thüringer Allgemeine Zeitung*'s headline on November 18, 1929, was "Erfurt commits moral suicide."[10]

The hatred and violence against Erfurt Jews in general and against Willi Wyjmoklyj's employer in particular must have made a deep impression on the adolescent Willi and been especially distressing. He was seventeen years old when the nationally distributed newspaper of the Central Association of German Citizens of Jewish Faith reported from Erfurt in 1926 that "Jewish pedestrians have been attacked by gangs of people

---

* Pun in the original German: *Erfurt, Erfurt—wir fürchten, mit diesem Manne ist auch deine Ehre fort.*

in broad daylight on their way to synagogue, . . . that Jewish citizens have had their windows smashed, . . . and that someone stabbed a Jewish lawyer in the back in the dark."[11] Willi Wyjmoklyj certainly must have followed the protest and the resistance on the part of the Jews, how the Erfurt Jewish community sued in court, took their complaints directly to the city council, and even repeatedly held protests,[12] and still encountered the superior power of their opponents with the electoral successes of the Schmalix forces, winning enough seats in 1932 that Thuringia became the first National Socialist-led state parliament, and finally Hitler's seizure of power in 1933.[13] It remains unknown why Willi was no longer employed at the Römischer Kaiser after he completed his apprenticeship in the autumn of 1928. In his curriculum vitae he mentions that after his apprenticeship he was "employed in several companies as a clerk." We have evidence that he continued to be employed in the textile trade.[14]

Surely he was aware how Schmalix's dystopias of hatred became reality under the National Socialist dictatorship and how the *Entjudung* (de-Jewing) of Erfurt was carried through to the bitter end. Shortly after the sixty-seven-year-old Pinthus died of a heart condition in 1937, his partner, Arndtheim, had to sign over the department store for a fraction of its worth to the limited partnership of Quehl & Co., headed by Hans Quehl from Leipzig.

"Mischling of the First Degree"

After the Nationalsozialistische Deutsche Arbeiterpartei (NSDAP) led by Adolf Hitler seized power in January 1933, Willy Wiemokli physically felt the consequences. So did his own family. The only reason was that they were increasingly excluded from society and persecuted on the basis of their Jewish religion or their Jewish roots.

The National Socialists invented a *deutsche Blut-und Volksgemeinschaft* (a German blood and folk community), from which they barred Jews as a "non-Aryan race." It made no difference whether someone identified as Jewish or whether they no longer believed in the Jewish faith of their forebears. At the beginning, the ideologues had difficulties themselves in establishing a demarcation line in order to say in whose veins "Jewish"—that is to say, "inferior" blood flowed.

Finally, the matter was codified in the Nuremberg Laws on September 15, 1935—the Reichsbürgergesetz (Reich Citizenship Law) and the Gesetz zum Schutz des deutschen Blutes und der deutschen Ehre (Law for the Protection of German Blood and Honor)—requiring that someone with "German blood" or an Aryan had to certify four non-Jewish grandparents; that is, four grandparents who did not belong to the Jewish religious community. Everyone else was a

Jew or a Mischling. Depending on parentage, a mixed-race person was a "half Jew"—designated as a "Mischling of the first degree" or a "quarter Jew"—designated as a "Mischling of the second degree." By means of these laws the National Socialists constructed a hierarchy with three levels: a Reich citizen was "a subject of the state who is of German or related blood," and had all the rights of a citizen of the state; state subjects of alien blood, such as German Jews or those who were certified as Jews, were declared to be "simple" national subjects with fewer rights; and legally below them were those Jews living in Germany without the status of being a state subject.

Willy's father, David Wiemokli, who was born in Berlin and had been a Protestant since 1908, was now considered a Jew on the basis of his four Jewish grandparents. And because his parents had immigrated from Poland to Germany, he was also legally a Polish national subject, not a German one. The so-called *Mischehe* (mixed marriage) with the "Aryan" Anna Wiemokli, which was counted as a "privileged Mischehe" on the basis that the child had been raised as a Protestant, was the only thing that provided David Wiemokli with some protection. But it is more than doubtful whether he could make a living as an independent shoe salesman or even earn an income. No doubt the boycotts against Jewish businesses that began in early 1933 also affected him. His son, Willy, wrote in 1949 that his father "had been unemployed and had no support since 1933."[1] David Wiemokli himself noted he had been without work since 1938.[2] A change in the commercial code banned Jews from jobs as salesmen effective October 1, 1938, and therefore from that date on he was explicitly prohibited from working.[3] It is unknown whether Anna Wiemokli could

Willy Wiemokli
E r f u r t
Gustav Adolfstr. 2a

4   15

L e b e n s l a u f

Ich wurde am 5.12.1908 in Halle/Saale als Sohn des kaufmännischen
Angestellten David Wiemokli und seiner Ehefrau Anna geb. Kaufmann
geboren. Ich besuchte die Oberrealschule in Erfurt bis zur Ober-
sekundareife und trat 1925 in das Kaufhaus Römischer Kaiser als
Lehrling ein. Nach beendeter Lehre war ich in mehreren Firman als
kaufm. Angestellter tätig.

Im Jahr 1938 wurde mein Vater und ich in das KZ Buchenwald gebracht
da mein Vater Jude und ich jüdischer Mischling war.

Nach der Rückehr aus dem KZ Buchenwald wurde ich aufgrund meiner
Inhaftierung von meinem damaligem Arbeitgeber Herrn Hans Türck
entlassen. Mein Vater war schon seit 1933 ohne Arbeit und ohne
Unterstützung. Es gelang mir aber 1939 wieder einen Arbeitsplatz
bei der Maschinenfabrik Topf & Söhne zu bekommen. in den Jahren
1939 bis 1944 wurde ich dreimal von der Gestapo in Haft wegen
Verdacht der Übertretung der Rassegesetze genommen. Es konnte mir
aber nichts nachgewiesen werden. An meinem Arbeitsplatz hatte ich
auch sehr unter der Gehässigkeit meiner Mitarbeiter zu leiden.

Im Jahr 1943 wurde mein Vater in das KZ A u s c h w i t z gebracht, in dem er bald nach seiner Einlieferung umgekommen sein
muß. Häftlingsnummer meines Vaters : 119684. Meine Mutter ist
bereits 1942 an einem Schlaganfall infolge der Aufregungen verstorben.

Im Jahr 1944 wurde ich von der Gestapo in eine Zwangsarbeitslager
bei Suhl gebracht und mit noch mehreren andern Erfurter Mischlin-
gen zusammen in einem Steinbruch zu schwerster Arbeit eingesetzt.
Nach erfolgter Befeiung durch die alliierten Truppen bin ich dann
wieder nach Erfurt zurückgekehrt.

Ich nahm sofort nach meiner Rückehr in meiner letzten Firma die
Arbeit wieder auf. Ich wurde in den Betriebsrat mit gewählt und
später als Sequester der Maschinenfabrik Topf & Söhne in Erfurt
eingesetzt. Nach Aufhebung der Seqestrierung war ich als Abteilungs
leiter und heute als Hauptbuchhalter tätig.

Ich versichere an Eides statt, daß vorstehende Angaben der Wahrheit
entsprechen.

Erfurt, den 13.1o.1949

Willy Wiemokli

*X Bei Topf und Söhne
wurden die Öfen für die Krematorien
in den KZ Lagern hergestellt.*

4. Curriculum vitae of Willy Wiemokli, October 13, 1949.
Wiemokli attached this to a questionnaire from the social welfare office of Erfurt, Department for the Victims of Fascism. The
handwritten note presumably made by office personnel reads, "X.
At Topf & Söhne the ovens were manufactured for the crematoria

(continued on facing page)

in the KZ-camps." LaTh-HStAW, Bezirkstag und Rat des Bezirkes Erfurt (District Assembly and Council of the District of Erfurt), VdN no. 3513, leaf 15r.

I was born in Halle/Saale on December 5, 1908, the son of the retail employee David Wiemokli and his wife Anna, née Kaufmann. I went to the secondary school in Erfurt until graduation and began my apprenticeship in the department store Römischer Kaiser in 1925. After completing my apprenticeship I worked at various companies as a retail employee.

In June of 1938, my father and I were taken to the KZ Buchenwald as my father was a Jew and I was a Jewish Mischling.

After returning from the KZ Buchenwald I was dismissed by my employer at the time Mr. Hans Türck on account of having been imprisoned. My father had been unemployed since 1933 and was without any support. I managed to find work in 1939 at the factory of Topf & Söhne. In the years between 1939 and 1944 I was arrested by the Gestapo three times on the suspicion of breaking the race laws. But nothing could be proven against me. At work I also had to suffer a lot from the nastiness of my coworkers.

In 1943 my father was taken to the KZ Auschwitz, where he must have died soon after his arrival. The prisoner number of my father: 119684. My mother had died of a stroke in 1942 as a result of agitation.

In 1944 I was taken to the forced labor camp near Suhl by the Gestapo and assigned to a quarry for hard labor together with other Erfurt Mischlinge. After my release due to the Allied troops, I returned to Erfurt.

After I returned, I immediately took up my job at my last company. I was voted onto the shop committee and later was made the sequestrator of the Topf & Söhne factory in Erfurt. After the end of the sequestration [forced receivership in the GDR under Soviet rule], I was the department head and am employed today the chief accountant.

I affirm in lieu of an oath that the above statement is true and correct.

Erfurt, October 13, 1949. [Signed] Willy Wiemokli

contribute to the support of the family. Certain, however, is the fact that her son supported the unemployed father.[4]

Mischlinge of the first degree like Willy Wiemokli continued to be Reich citizens, just with fewer rights than citizens of "German blood." They could never be sure that they too would not become the object of National Socialist persecution. For example, starting a family was extremely difficult for them under the Nuremberg Laws. If Willy Wiemokli, who was twenty-six at the time and had been employed for several years after successfully completing his apprenticeship, were to marry a Jewish woman, his status as a Mischling of the first degree would mean that he and his children would be classified as Jews and would be persecuted. At the same time "adulterous sex"—that is, a romantic relationship with a non-Jewish woman—was forbidden and punishable as *Rassenschande* (race pollution). Theoretically, marrying a non-Jew was possible with special permission; in practice, it was out of the question.

In Buchenwald

In 1938 the National Socialists began mass arrests of people who were in the Jewish community or had Jewish roots. For Jews of Polish citizenship in Germany (there were at least sixty thousand)[1] the situation was even more precarious. They were to be expelled like all other Jews from Germany by the Nazis, but the Polish government feared the return of these refugees, who had been deprived of their subsistence. On March 31, 1938, the Polish parliament passed a law aimed directly at these refugees that enabled the Polish government to strip Polish citizens of their citizenship if they had continuously lived abroad for five years or more. Implementing this provision was arbitrary and filled with delays. At first, the measure was enforced only if the person in question applied for a Polish passport or wanted it extended.[2] Apparently this is what happened with David Wiemokli when he had a foreigner's passport issued to him by German authorities on July 4, 1938. This was the identity pass replacement for a foreigner who could not get the document from his or her own country or who was stateless. A decree by the Polish interior ministry on October 6 ordered every Polish citizen abroad to register his or her passport at the appropriate consulate and, further, that the document would become invalid on October 29 without the official stamp.[3] The

21

German authorities then did exactly what the Polish government had wanted to prevent—on short notice they deported to Poland over seventeen thousand Jews with Polish citizenship who were living in Germany—who, like David Wiemokli, had long been living in Germany. The police began mass arrests on October 27, and by October 29 everyone was supposed to have crossed the Germany-Poland border. In this number were also eighty-one Erfurt inhabitants, including two Aryan wives who had taken the Polish citizenship of their husbands.[4] David Wiemokli was probably not affected by this deportation only because he was in a Mischehe. That he was trying to remain as invisible as possible to the persecutors can be seen when comparing Erfurt's official address books. In the address book from 1938, the name David Wiemokli disappears for the first time and then is absent in the following years. Only Willy Wiemokli still appears as head of household for the address they shared (see table, p. 8).

On November 7, 1938, the teenager Herschel Grynszpan, whose family from Hannover had been caught up in the forced deportation across the Polish border, assassinated the German legation secretary Ernst vom Rath in Paris. The NSDAP leadership immediately decided to carry out an organized, statewide pogrom against German Jews, labeled as revenge for Rath's death. Coordinated by the state, members of the SA and SS set synagogues on fire across all of Germany in the night from November 9 to November 10. In Erfurt, the synagogue at Karthäuserring 14, dedicated in 1884, was totally destroyed. The synagogue built in 1952 at this address (today Max-Cars-Platz 1) is the only postwar construction of a synagogue in the German Democratic Republic. After the pogrom, the Jewish community had to pay for the demolition of the burnt-out ruin as well as the gasoline for the arson. Altogether, an "expiation fine" of a billion reichsmarks* was imposed on the Jews in Germany. The SS and SA troops plundered and destroyed some 7,500 Jewish-owned businesses throughout Germany. They dragged some thirty thousand Jewish men from their homes and beat and abused them. About one hundred of them were killed that night.

Among the 183 men arrested in Erfurt herded into the high school gymnasium and registered with the criminal police or the Gestapo was Willy Wiemokli.[5] Toward three in the morning he arrived in the very room where he had had sport classes as a youth and became the fifty-fifth detainee registered.[6] The laconic phrase "beatings in the high school," used by Wiemokli in October 1945 to describe his hours in the gymnasium, glosses over the abuse of the detainees with batons, whips, iron dumbbells, and on the sport equipment, all accompanied by the deafening bellowing of drunken SA and SS men.[7] Toward six o'clock buses drove them to Buchenwald.[8] Willy Wiemokli, the person, turned into Buchenwald Prisoner no. 20619, assigned to Block 50 of the *Pogromsonderlager* (special pogrom camp).[9]

Two questions arise from his arrest. Why was Willi Wyjmoklyj even arrested when this terror action wasn't aimed at half Jews, and among the ten thousand men imprisoned in Buchenwald only a few were half Jews?[10] And why is his father missing from the list with 183 names made that night in the

---

* About US$400 million in 1938.

5. High school gymnasium, Erfurt, 1911. StadtA Erfurt 6-0/9G13_057.

gymnasium? Instead, David Wyjmoklyj was put on two short lists with only eight or nine names.[†] The first list is captioned "Arrested in Erfurt" and has a handwritten note, "von Abtlg. III aufgenommen, von St[apo] Erfurt nicht abgegeben" (taken by Dept. III, not handed over by St[ate police] Erfurt) with the date November 18, 1938. The abbreviation *Ha* below this

---

[†] For the English translation, Annegret Schüle revised numbers and clarified names on the arrest lists in the text and endnotes. The author has also revised the names of the archives for her sources to reflect recent changes.

notice shows that the signer was Hermann Hackmann, the second commander of the *Schutzhaftlager* (protective custody camp) of the KZ Buchenwald. He is saying that these men were recorded in Buchenwald but weren't on the Erfurt Gestapo's list with the 183 men. By "not handed over," SS usage meant not the delivered men, but only that they were listed on the paperwork that accompanied them. Hackmann noted on the list with the 183 names, "Lager/nach Erfurt Liste senden da n[icht] volls[tändig] Ha 10.11.38" (Camp/send list to Erfurt since n[ot] comp[lete] Ha November 10, 1938). Hackmann's two notes acknowledge that it had to have been David Wyjmoklyj and the other seven men in the buses from Erfurt who arrived in Buchenwald on the morning of November 10, but that he certainly hadn't been taken with his son to the gymnasium at three in the morning. Apparently David Wyjmoklyj was arrested later that morning and then—perhaps without ever having been in the gymnasium—transported to Buchenwald with the men who were being held there and others who had been rounded up. There, in Buchenwald, Hackmann ascertained that the long list was incomplete (which he noted on the list on November 10). In Buchenwald the aforementioned list with the caption "Arrested in Erfurt" was now drawn up with the eight names, including David Wyjmoklyj's. This list was edited with the handwritten note by Hackmann on November 18—to account for the existence of these eight men.

Of the 183 men registered in the gymnasium only 179 were taken to Buchenwald; four were no longer capable of being transported. Another eight men were in the transport without having first been registered in the gymnasium as evidenced by the list with eight names. Two more Erfurt men must be counted who were missing from this list but are named on the list with nine people. Although this list is captioned "Secret State Police, State Police Station Erfurt" and is dated "Erfurt, November 11," all the men named here must have been on the transport the morning of November 10 for two reasons. Other sources from Buchenwald show that they were there. And there was no transport from Erfurt to Buchenwald on November 11. Therefore, it must have been 189 Erfurt men who came to Buchenwald on the morning of November 10, 1938, including father and son Wyjmoklyj.[11]

Apparently the Gestapo encountered Willy Wiemokli in the apartment at Gustav-Adolf-Strasse 2a as the only male resident there. It is unknown if his father was also in the apartment and had been able to hide. The Gestapo arrested the son Willy so they could check off the name Wyjmoklyj on their list. Under circumstances that cannot be tracked down now, they could also have picked up David later.

David Wiemokli was sixty-three years old when he and his son had to suffer hunger, thirst, crowding, lack of sleep, constant threats, and torments by the SS in Buchenwald. Over 250 inmates died in this *Sonderlager* (special camp), including four men from Erfurt. On November 26, 1938, David and Willy Wiemokli were released.[12] Willy Wiemokli's then-current employer in Erfurt, Hans Türck, a merchant we assume was living at Jägerstrasse 16, would no longer employ him.[13] That Willy was employed there as a sales assistant was already a sign of lowered status since the address book for the city of Erfurt labels him as a "salesman" until 1936.[14]

At Topf & Söhne

One can imagine Willy Wiemokli's relief and gratitude when he was able to find a job as an accountant at the prestigious engineering works of J. A. Topf & Söhne in January 1939—even though he "came from the textile branch, that is to say, a different branch." When the business director Ernst Wolfgang Topf employed him, he knew that Willy Wiemokli had been imprisoned in Buchenwald as a "Jewish Mischling."[1]

It was at this very concentration camp that the firm of Topf & Söhne delivered its first mobile cremation oven toward the end of 1939, after approximately eight hundred of some three thousand inmates—Viennese Jews and non-Jewish Poles—had died in a second *Sonderlager* built after the beginning of the war.

The SS had beaten the prisoners, let them starve, freeze, or die in the dysentery epidemic that had swept through the camp. The engineer for this cremation oven and all other ovens set up in the camp by the firm of Topf & Söhne was Kurt Prüfer.[2]

Kurt Prüfer received 2 percent commission of the gross profit of all the sales he generated. In order to claim his commission, Prüfer had to document his sales with an accurate list of purchasers and the amount of the order. It was the task of Willy Wiemokli, as the colleague in the accounting

6. J. A. Topf & Söhne's administrative building, 1940. LaTh-HStAW, J. A. Topf & Söhne no. 296, leaf 30r.

department, to reconcile Prüfer's claims against the information from accounting. Due to these lists it is certain that Wiemokli knew that Topf & Söhne accepted orders for Buchenwald, Dachau, Mauthausen, Auschwitz, Flossenbürg, and Sachsenhausen, and was doing business directly with the SS-Hauptamt für Haushalt und Bauten Berlin (SS Central Office, Department of Budget and Buildings Berlin), the top construction authority for the concentration camps. What must have gone through Willy Wiemokli's mind when he noted in red pencil that the contract 41D80 with the SS New Building Management for Mauthausen for over 9,003 reichsmarks—a fixed double-muffle incineration oven—had been listed twice by Kurt Prüfer?[3]

7. Sales list of Kurt Prüfer, Department D IV, January–March 1941. The checkmarks, asterisks, swirls, and notes are Willy Wiemokli's marks. LaTh-HStAW, J. A. Topf & Söhne no. 14, leaf 111r.

On August 2, 1941, Willy Wiemokli noted that Kurt Prüfer had claimed an excess of 111,954 reichsmarks in sales for the years 1936–41. The difference was basically due to Kurt Prüfer taking the signed contract as the basis of what he listed, and not the delivered and invoiced amount (i.e., the products charged to the account).[4] In March 1941 the Topf brothers had cancelled their commission agreement with Prüfer. In its place he received an increase in salary, which amounted to 5.6 percent if one includes his previous commissions. Kurt Prüfer now no longer had to keep these sales lists and Willy Wiemokli no longer had to review them. However, it can be assumed that through his work Willy Wiemokli continued to know about business dealings with the SS, including equipping Auschwitz-Birkenau with large crematoria in 1942 and 1943.[5]

Love

Sometime after 1934 Willy Wiemokli met Erika Glass, who was five years younger than he. Like him, she had finished her schooling with the tenth grade and was also employed in retail. The young woman came from Eisenach and had been living in Erfurt since 1934. Here she worked in the well-known fashion house Reibstein on Junkersand Street, and was very successful in her career. This "Thuringian House of Fashion and Accoutrements" was a serious competitor of the Römischer Kaiser department store. In November 1944 it was partially destroyed by a direct bomb hit. Today at the same address is the fashion house Breuninger. At Reibstein, Erika Glass was promoted to buyer and manager of the fashion goods department.[1] She wasn't Jewish and therefore her relationship with Willy Wiemokli counted as *Rassenschande*. Even a kiss or other public display of affection could mean a prison sentence of several years for him and a public shaming for her. Comparable examples show that non-Jewish women in such cases even faced being sent to a concentration camp.

Three times the Gestapo held Willy Wiemokli for several days in 1942 and 1943 because they suspected him of "forbidden contact."[2] The denunciations came from colleagues. Willy Wiemokli claims that Ernst Wolfgang Topf "tried

Erika Wiemokli

3. 1. 1984

50 Erfurt
Prager Straße 11/87

Lebenslauf.

Ich wurde am 8.6.1913 in Eisenach geboren und besuchte dort die Schule bis zur Mittl. Reif (heute 10 Klassenschule)! Anschließend habe ich in der Bausparkasse Thüringia 1931 - 1932 als kaufm. männliche Angestellte gelernt. Der Betrieb machte pleite und ich war stellungslos! (mit 80.- Gehalt)

1934 ging ich nach Erfurt zur Fa. Reibstein und war dort in verschiedenen Abteilungen tätig, habe mich hoch gearbeitet bis zur Einkäuferin und Leiterin der Stoff-Modewaren!

Durch den Krieg wurde ich 1944 noch in die heutige Optima verpflichtet bis ich 1945 wegen Arbeitsmängel entlassen wurde!

Im September heiratete mich Willy Wiemokli mit dem ich vorher nur illegal Verbindung hatte, da er Jüdischer Mischling war! War jetzt nur Hausfrau!

Ab Oktober 1953 war ich wieder tätig, in der Sozial Versitung als Buchhalterin, mußte aber aus gesundheitlichen Gründen die Tätigkeit 1954 wieder aufgeben, da mein Mann Pflege brauchte!

Erika Wiemokli

8. Curriculum vitae of Erika Wiemokli, January 3, 1984. Erika Wiemokli attached this to her application for recognition as the surviving dependent of a Persecuted Person of the Nazi Regime.

(continued on facing page)

LaTh-HStAW, Bezirkstag und Rat des Bezirkes Erfurt (District Assembly and Council of the District of Erfurt), VdN no. 3513, leaf 26r.

Curriculum vitae

I was born in Eisenach on June 8, 1913, and went to school there through the Mittlere Reife (today the tenth grade)! Immediately after leaving school, I was apprenticed at the savings bank Thuringia in 1931–1932 as a commercial employee. The business went bankrupt and I was unemployed!

In 1934 I went to Erfurt to the company Reibstein (with a salary of 80 [marks]) and was employed there in various departments, worked my way up to buyer and manager of the fashion goods department!

Because of the war I was also obligated in 1944 to work at today's Optima [a manufacturer of precision mechanics] until 1945 when I was let go because of lack of work.

In September Willy Wiemokli married me, with whom I only had an illegal connection because he was a Jewish Mischling! Was only a housewife at first!

Starting in October 1953 I was employed again as a bookkeeper with the social insurance office, but had to give up the job in 1954 for health reasons because my husband needed care!

Erika Wiemokli

everything" at the time to free him from detention, and had personally gone to the Gestapo.[3] Wiemokli actually got off comparatively lightly. He avoided prison or even a sentence to a concentration camp.

Willy Wiemokli and his girlfriend were steadfast in their relationship; they did not allow their own fear or the anti-Semitic hostility around them destroy their bond.

Over the years, Erika Glass accepted the danger the relationship brought with it, the illegality and forced concealment. She waited until she was thirty-two, when Wiemokli, thirty-six, could marry her, four months after the end of the war, on September 8, 1945. The late marriage possibly accounted for the fact that they had no children. Their marriage lasted for thirty-eight years, until Willy Wiemokli died in 1983.[4]

Father's Deportation and Murder

Jews, or those who were considered to be Jews, who, like David Wiemokli, lived with Aryan partners in a Mischehe were at first spared deportation from the German Reich into the death camps in the East.[1] In 1938 Hitler personally divided Mischehen into "privileged" and "nonprivileged" unions, even if this was never codified into law.[2] The Wiemoklis's marriage counted as a "privileged Mischehe" because, although he was considered a Jew, the father and his wife had a child, Willy Wiemokli, who had not been raised Jewish. "Privileged" meant that the person was spared various restrictions imposed on Jews. This meant, for example, that the Wiemoklis were allowed to stay in their home and did not have to move to a Jews' house, and eventually the existing assets could be transferred to the Aryan partner or child.[3] In addition, Jews in "privileged mixed marriages" were exempt from the requirement to wear the *Judenstern* (yellow star) that singled out any Jew over the age of six.[4] Even when those Jews living in "privileged mixed marriages" were under duress and also found themselves increasingly targeted by the regime, many owed their survival to the delay that arose from their status.[5]

The Wiemoklis, like others in Erfurt, also watched the first deportation of Erfurt's Jews on May 9, 1942, which was followed by more. One hundred one people, the youngest four years old, were told to gather at the main train station and were first taken to Weimar and then to the Bełżyce ghetto set up by the Germans near Lublin. Not a single person survived. By the end of the war there were only a few spouses living in mixed marriage in the city out of 1,290 Jews who had belonged to the Erfurt Jewish community in January 1932 before the National Socialist persecution began. Many had emigrated, many had even committed suicide, and of those who had been deported to the camps almost no one survived.[6]

On June 14, 1942, five weeks after the deportations from Erfurt began, Anna Wiemokli, age fifty-six, died "of a stroke due to agitation," as her son euphemistically described the anti-Semitic repression against her family and the stress of persecution.[7] With his wife's death, David Wiemokli lost the protection of a "privileged mixed marriage" and was now completely exposed to the racist forces of annihilation. At the end of December 1942 he had to extend his residence permit and apply for a new alien's passport. The first alien's passport of July 1938 had apparently expired. To do so, he went to the second district police station in Erfurt. There the police officer noticed that the old passport had been issued to "Wyjmoklyj, David, Israel," but the passport holder had signed only "David Wyjmoklyj" and, moreover, he had also signed his new applications for the alien's passport and the residence permit without the legally required additional name of Israel. "It should be reviewed as to whether W. as a stateless [sic!] Jew is obligated to also use the name of Israel when signing documents," this policeman, by the name of Wedemann, inquired of the police commissioner on December 30, 1942. The answer came on January 5, 1943, that David Wyjmoklyj was required after January 1, 1939, to add the given name of Israel, and that he was also required to give notice of this to the local police authorities where he lived, the civil authorities of the place where he was born, and the civil authorities where his marriage took place—as required of all Jews. Therefore a criminal charge was to be filed against him. David Wyjmoklyj was summoned to a hearing for January 11. At this hearing he testified that he had not registered the additional given name because he "had nothing to do with the Jewish community" since his marriage, "had received no notice of this requirement" and, furthermore, had "read nothing about this in the newspapers." He had unintentionally omitted Israel on both new applications. He would undertake that day to notify all authorities. He signed this testimony with "David Israel Wyjmoklyj."[8] The requirement to add the name Israel was in fact put into effect only after the first alien's passport had been issued. Perhaps David Wyjmoklyj really did not know of the requirement to subsequently file with the authorities and he certainly did not want any more contact with state authorities than absolutely necessary. That he left out Israel on the new applications could be due to lack of habit. Over the last years he had withdrawn from society as much as possible to protect himself—shielded by his wife and supported by his son.

On January 12 the police issued a charge against David Wyjmoklyj; on February 15 the magistrate's court issued an order of punishment for violating paragraphs 1–4 of the Second Decree on the Execution of the Law Regarding the Changing of Surnames and Forenames of August 17, 1938.[9] David Wyjmoklyj's punishment was a prison sentence of one month and a fee of ten reichsmarks, paid on March 5. On March 17 he began his sentence in the prison on Andreasstrasse 35 (where today there is a memorial and education center with a focus on the GDR dictatorship and its Staatssicherheit (Stasi or State Security).[10] On March 24 the Erfurt field office of the Gestapo in Weimar requested a copy of the order of punishment in duplicate from the magistrate's court. In the case of criminal offenses, cooperation between the justice system and the Gestapo was particularly close.[11] Ludwig Hüttig, then thirty-two years old and director or acting director of the Erfurt field office, signed the request to the magistrate's court. Hüttig, a native of Thuringia, was a pastor's son, had broken off his theological studies in Jena, and had been employed by the Gestapo since 1936.[12] On April 17 David Wyjmoklyj was supposed to be released after completing his sentence. The day before, he was taken from the prison at two o'clock by the Gestapo and deported to Auschwitz.[13]

On May 1, 1943, the sixty-six-year-old David Wiemokli arrived in Auschwitz-Birkenau, and received his inmate number, 119684.[14] He survived only eleven weeks. The fact that he was assigned a number means that he was not sent to the gas chamber for extermination on his arrival, but was first assigned to forced labor. At his age this would have been unusual. The question whether conditions of the camp killed him or if he was murdered outright cannot be determined now. However, his body was definitely burned in an oven made by J. A. Topf & Söhne. According to the death certificate of Auschwitz's registry office document, the camp's physician, Obersturmführer Friedrich Entress, certified that David Wyjmoklyj died at 5:50 p.m. on July 18, 1943. Entress was in charge of the prison hospital in the Buna/Monowitz concentration camp

15 15

Strafgefängnis Erfurt	Erfurt, den 16.April 43 19

Gefgb. Nr.: 1028/42
(bei allen Schreiben anzugeben)

Zum dortigen Geschäftszeichen:
8 Cs.34/43

A.G.Erfurt

Fernruf: Hausanschl.

An

das Amtsgericht

in Erfurt

17 APRIL 1943

Mitteilung des Abganges eines Gefangenen oder Verwahrten
(Nrn. 207 Abs. 1, 208 Abs. 3 VollzO)

Familienname:	Wyjmoklyj	Rassen- bzw. Volkszugehörigkeit:	
(bei Frauen auch Geburtsname)			
Rufname:	David Israel	Familienstand:	verw.
Zuletzt ausgeübter Beruf:	Kaufmann	Zahl der Kinder:	eins
Geburtstag:	13.10.1876	Letzte Wohnung vor der Aufnahme zum Vollzuge:	
Geburtsort:	Berlin	Erfurt,Gustav Adolfstr.2 2 a	
Staatsangehörigkeit:	J u d e		

ist am 16. April 19 43 14 Uhr 00 in der Sache wegen Nichtführen des Vornamen
- Israel-
entlassen — und — von der Gestapo abgeholt ~~xxxxxxxxxxxxxxxx~~ — worden —

~~xxxxxxxxxx~~
~~xxxxxxxxxxxxx~~ —.
Geschäftszeichen:

beabsichtigt in

Wohnung zu nehmen.

Grund des Abganges: Ablauf einer Gefängnisstrafe von 1 Monat.

Name:

Amtsbezeichnung:

VollzO. A 27 Mitteilung des Abganges.
Druckerei Zuchthaus Stein (Donau) Q 0949

9. City prison of Erfurt, Notice of a Prisoner or Detainee Departure, April 16, 1943. This is the last trace of David Wiemokli in his native city of Erfurt. Original: LA Thüringen-Staatsarchiv Gotha, Amtsgericht Erfurt (Magistrate's Court Erfurt) no. 1006, leaf 15.

and was known as being especially brutal. After the war survivors testified that he selected sick prisoners for murder and lethal experiments with typhus. According to the death certificate David Israel Wyjmoklyj's cause of death was "myocardial degeneration with phlegmon," a very painful inflammation of connective tissue caused by an external wound, treatable with antibiotics, but can cause fatal blood poisoning if left untreated. This cause of death is most certainly a fabrication; we know the usual practice was that the prisoner clerk in the hospital chose this or some other diagnosis from a list provided by the SS doctors in order to conceal from the family the suffering and violent death of their relatives.

David Wyjmoklyj's death certificate, dated July 30, 1943, was signed by SS-Untersturmführer Maximilian Grabner, the director of the political department in the camp complex of Auschwitz. The civil registry office, along with all five crematoria, was under his management. In the main camp's crematoria three double-muffle ovens of J. A. Topf & Söhne were still in operation until the end of July 1943 before the incineration of the corpses was organized in four large crematoria, also fitted with Topf & Söhne ovens, in the extermination camp of Birkenau. That Grabner correctly had written on the death certificate "Protestant, formerly Mosaic" (i.e., Jewish) contradicts in an absurd way the National Socialist idea that David Israel Wyjmoklyj was exterminated because he was a Jew.[15]

David's sister, Sara Gans, Willy Wiemokli's aunt living in Berlin, was also deported to Auschwitz in 1943 and murdered there.[16] There were also others in Erfurt who had lost the protection of their Mischehe through the death of their spouse or divorce and were deported; after 1944 even Jewish partners in intact mixed marriages, along with their children, were deported.[17] Willy Wiemokli was fortunate that he didn't share his father's fate.

He remained behind in the three-room apartment at Gustav-Adolf-Strasse 2a on his own, where he had moved with

Nr. 25587/1943   C¹

Auschwitz, den 30. Juli _____ 1943

D er Kaufmann David Israel Wyjmoklyj _____

_____, evangelisch früher mosaisch,

wohnhaft Erfurt, Gustav-Adolfstrasse Nr. 2 A _____,

ist am 18. Juli 1943 _____ um 17 Uhr 50 Minuten

in Auschwitz, Kasernenstrasse _____ verstorben.

D er Verstorbene war geboren am 13. Oktober 1876 _____

in Berlin _____

(Standesamt _____ Nr. _____)

Vater: Nochman Wyjmoklyj _____

Mutter: Estra Wyjmoklyj geborene Wyssnowicz _____

D er Verstorbene war — nicht — verheiratet Witwer von Anna Wyjmoklyj
geborene Kaufmann _____

Eingetragen auf mündliche — schriftliche Anzeige des Arztes Doktor der
Medizin Entress in Auschwitz vom 18. Juli 1943 _____

D er Anzeigende _____

Vorgelesen-genehmigt und _____ unterschrieben.

Die Übereinstimmung mit dem
Zweitbuch wird beglaubigt.

Auschwitz, den 30. 7. 1943

Der Standesbeamte   Der Standesbeamte
In Vertretung   In Vertretung
         Grabner

Todesursache: Herzmuskeldegeneration bei Phlegmone

Eheschließung d Verstorbenen am _____ in _____

Standesamt _____ Nr. _____

10. Death certificate of David Wyjmoklyj, issued by the civil registry office of the Auschwitz concentration camp, July 30, 1943. ITS Digital Archive, Bad Arolsen, 1.1.21/629198.

his parents many years before. It could be that his job at Topf & Söhne became even more important to him after losing both his mother and father and in the face of the threat hanging over him even though—as he reported later—he suffered "a lot from the nastiness" from his coworkers.[18]

Forced-Labor Camp

When the deportations to extermination camps began across the Third Reich in October 1941, the discussion among the power elite recommenced about how to handle a Jewish Mischling of the first degree; those of the second degree were not targeted for persecution because their blood was predominantly Aryan, as long as they had no connection with Jews. The controversy was basically between the top Nazi Party functionaries and the interior and justice ministries: the party functionaries considered a "final solution to the Jewish question" only required murdering mixed-race Jews or Mischlinge of the first degree; the ministries favored a slow "natural extinction" by forcibly sterilizing those of mixed blood rather than immediate annihilation. At the Wannsee Conference, as the meeting of leading party and ministerial officials on January 20, 1942, came to be known, in which the organizational measures for the destruction of European Jews were decided, the "Mischling questions" loomed large. The position of the top party officials as outlined in the minutes basically wanted to consider Mischlinge as Jews to be murdered: "persons of mixed blood of the first degree . . . will, as regards the final solution of the Jewish question, be treated as Jews." Despite further consultation, they were unable to come to a final agreement on a course of action.[1] It is only for this reason that many of these people survived the National Socialist regime.

Because Jewish Mischlinge were drafted until they were barred from military service in 1940, there were plans in the works to assign them instead to work battalions.[2] In 1944 all Mischlinge of the first degree were drafted for forced labor in the Todt Organization, an enormous construction organization within the arms ministry using concentration camp inmates, prisoners of war, and forced laborers from occupied countries. Their work was intended to extend a war that was long since no longer winnable. They were primarily used to build military facilities as well as infrastructure for the war, the most famous example being the West Wall on the French-German border.[3] The gauleiter of Thuringia, Fritz Sauckel, as the general plenipotentiary for labor deployment, took over implementing the forced-labor brigades of Mischlinge.[4] Even though the forced recruitment began slowly, ten to twenty thousand Mischlinge of the first degree, who were "subject to special service," were seized and delivered into the camps of the Todt Organization by the fall of 1944. There they had to work under conditions comparable to those in the concentration camps. Far too heavy work and mistreatment by the guards was the routine day after day.[5]

With others from Erfurt, Willy Wiemokli was taken to a forced-labor camp on October 16, 1944, in Suhl, where, according to his own testimony, he was compelled to perform "very heavy work" in a quarry.[6] For a while he was also in a labor camp in Eisenach.[7] Previously, Ernst Wolfgang Topf had been able to prevent Wiemokli from being called up by the labor office or by the war-related production office for forced labor, according to the testimony of company's head secretary after the war. Even now Topf fought for Wiemokli, but without success, as Wiemokli stated in his sworn statement after the war.[8]

Back at Topf & Söhne

After being freed by the US Army on April 3, 1945, Willy Wiemokli returned to Erfurt and, as he wrote in his curriculum vitae, "immediately" went back to work at Topf & Söhne.[1] After August 1945 we know he was a member and the recording secretary of the shop committee; he had possibly been on the committee in the previous months. From the beginning of November 1945, the shop committee was headed by Friedrich Schiller, a boilermaker and member of the KPD (Communist Party of Germany) since its founding in 1919. In the shop committee Heinrich Messing was also active at first before he took a job in July 1945 with the Erfurt criminal police. Messing, who had even spent eleven weeks under arrest in "protective custody" in 1933, was the mechanic who had been sent to install the ventilation in the gas chambers in Auschwitz-Birkenau in 1943, and had been present when they were put into operation, meaning he witnessed a mass killing using Zyklon B. It is not known if Willy Wiemokli was present at the shop committee's meeting on April 27, 1945, when Ludwig Topf, Ernst Wolfgang Topf's brother and technical manager of the company, spoke with the members about the oven deliveries to the concentration camps. Ludwig Topf mentioned only Buchenwald by name and justified the company's cooperation with the SS by explaining that burning the corpses had "absolutely [corresponded] to hygienic demands." The members of the shop committee agreed with this statement and assured Ludwig Topf that he did not need "to harbor any misgivings."[2]

The company management and the shop committee hoped that after the end of the National Socialist regime business done with the SS would have no consequences—that did not happen. On the morning of May 31, 1945, Ludwig Topf committed suicide by poison at his home at Hirnzigenweg 18 to avoid arrest by the US Army Counter Intelligence Corps (CIC). Kurt Prüfer had been arrested the day before, after the US Army had stumbled across the Topf & Söhne ovens in Buchenwald's crematorium. However, he was released fourteen days later. After Ludwig Topf's death his brother, Ernst Wolfgang, traveled to the occupation zones in the West to collect his brother's life insurance there. Ernst Topf was unable to return after the Soviet Army took over Thuringia on July 3, 1945. Now the company was considered "unowned" and was placed under a sequestrator, as an official receiver is known, designated by SMAD (Soviet Military Administration of Germany). The official receiver at first was Kurt Schmidt, the department manager for silo construction. He had been appointed proxy by Ernst Wolfgang Topf before he had left and was confirmed by SMAD as the sequestrator with the authority to manage the company.[3]

Loyalty

Willy Wiemokli was, as was the entire shop committee, in favor of giving the company back to the Topf family. The sworn statement that Wiemokli gave for Ernst Wolfgang Topf on December 28, 1945, aimed to do so.[1] It is understandable that for him a good relationship to his employer was more important than opposition to doing business with the SS—as long as the Damocles sword of National Socialist persecution was hanging over him. It is hard to understand, however, when the anti-Semitic dictatorship ended that he did not take the opportunity to call to account the accomplices in the genocide of the Jews in his own company. It is improbable that Willy Wiemokli, who certainly knew early on of the business relationship with the SS and also later as an employee in the company's accounting department, didn't have insider knowledge about the company providing engineering expertise to Auschwitz for working the gas chambers and crematoria to handle the murder victims. It seems as if—after living with all the ostracism and threats—the desire to belong, to be permitted to contribute professionally, and to have responsibility had been the deciding factors. And it is clear that he remained connected to Ernst Wolfgang Topf by deep gratitude even after 1945 because Topf had afforded Willy protection when a colleague had denounced him to the Gestapo or when he had been called up for forced labor. Wiemokli's loyalty was not only to his former boss but also to his colleagues who had participated in the business with the SS, as well as to the company itself.

Immediately after the war the shop committees were far more than just entities that represented workers' interests. They saw themselves as responsible for rebuilding the economy. At the top of their concerns was starting up production again. Also important was that the company rid itself of any National Socialists who could "sabotage . . . the effort to rebuild."[2] When the longtime foreman Hugo Liebeskind, for example, inquired in February 1946 if his son just released from prison could be hired, the shop committee declined, saying, "Karl Liebeskind was generally known as a Nazi true believer."[3] Meanwhile, Willy Wiemokli was the representative of the shop committee whenever the Communist president was away and, at the beginning of 1946, he even joined the KPD. When the KPD and SPD (Socialist Party of Germany) merged and became the SED (Sozialistische Einheitspartei Deutschlands, or Socialist Unity Party of Germany) in the Soviet Occupation Zone in April 1946, Wiemokli became a member.[4] He not only shared persecution under National Socialism and the desire to build a new, anti-fascist society with his comrades at work, he also shared the knowledge of the company's complicity in the mass destruction of human life in Auschwitz and their own involvement. The Communist Heinrich Messing and the "half Jew" Wiemokli could have each suppressed in similar fashion their own, different sort of complicity in National Socialism—both men rejected the National Socialist system, both had suffered incarceration in a camp, both had found safe harbor in a company that was not run by Nazis.

There, both men had "only" done their job duties correctly and conscientiously, be it reviewing the orders of oven deliveries for the concentration camps or technically optimizing the gas chambers.

At the Head of the Company

On March 4, 1946, four managing engineers at Topf & Söhne were arrested by officers of the counterintelligence agency of the Soviet army, SMERSH (SMERt SHpionam; in English, death to spies): Kurt Prüfer, the engineer who installed all the crematoria delivered to the concentration camps; Karl Schultze, responsible for the ventilation in the gas chambers in Auschwitz-Birkenau; Fritz Sander, supervisor of these two engineers; and Gustav Braun, who had been responsible for production in the entire company for ten years. From a report by an investigative committee on Auschwitz-Birkenau, the Soviet authorities had known since May 1945 of the role of the company of Topf & Söhne in the death factories of the extermination camps. When the sequestrator Kurt Schmidt learned of the arrests, under the pretext of taking sick leave he preferred to flee to the West with his wife rather than return to his position at the company. Once again the company lacked someone at the helm.

Willy Wiemokli, who had already taken over the duties of Kurt Schmidt after Gustav Braun's arrest, offered to become the new sequestrator. The nomination came from Friedrich Schiller, the Communist shop committee president. Wiemokli was unanimously supported by the shop committee and by the company's *Prokuristen* (authorized legal representatives), such as the salesman Max Machemehl, who had participated in the business with Auschwitz before 1945 but had successfully concealed his complicity until now from the Soviet investigators. To become the sequestrator, Wiemokli resigned his position as member of the shop committee on March 28, 1946.

As a member of the shop committee and then as the sequestrator, Wiemokli worked closely with Friedrich Schiller. In March 1946 he in turn had advised Heinrich Messing, the man who had installed the ventilation in Auschwitz, to avoid arrest by going into hiding when the four engineers had been taken away by the Soviet officers. Willy Wiemokli and Friedrich Schiller were temporarily not only the most powerful men in the company, but after August 1946 they both also lived for a time in the company villa on Hirnzigenweg 18, empty since Ludwig Topf's death.[1]

As one of his first official acts as sequestrator, Wiemokli had to clarify whether the wives of the four engineers arrested at the beginning of March 1946 should continue to receive money from the company. After talking with the shop committee, the March salary was to be paid in full, and also a large part of the April salary, designated as "advanced payment." In mid-May 1946 the FDGB (Freier Deutscher Gewerkschaftsbund, or Free German Trade Union Federation) demanded that the four men be fired without notice and forbade any further payments to the wives. The company would otherwise be "suspected of preferential treatment."[2] Despite the implied threat Wiemokli did not fire the four arrested men and successfully challenged the FDGB so that the wives of "our arrested men" could receive a monthly payment to not "be in distress."[3] In 1946 he also paid all managing employees the

Erfurt, den 28. Mai 1946
Wiem./schü.

Aktennotiz
von Herrn Wiemokli

Betrifft: Gehaltszahlung unserer inhaftierten Herren

Aufgrund der telefonischen Auskunft, dass keine Gehaltszahlungen an die
inhaftierten Gefolgschaftsmitglieder zu zahlen sind, habe ich mich noch-
mals mit dem Sekretariat des F.D.G.B. in Verbindung gesetzt und die Sach-
lage besprochen. Da eine direkte rechtliche Forderung der Frauen
n i c h t besteht, ist Herr Fechtner des F.D.G.B. auch der Meinung, dass
wir eine Vorschußzahlung leisten können, die später mit dem Gehalt wieder aufgerechnet werden kann, damit die Ehefrauen der inhaftierten Gefolgschaftsmitglieder nicht in eine Notlage geraten.

Wir werden deshalb weiterhin die monatlichen Unterstützungszahlungen
bis zu einer endgültigen Entscheidung zahlen.

1 Kopie Pers.Akte Sander
1 Kopie Pers.Akte Braun
1 Kopie Pers.Akte Prüfer
1 Kopie Pers.Akte Schulze

11. "Salary Paid to Our Imprisoned Men," Memo to file by Willy
Wiemokli, in the personnel file of Kurt Prüfer, May 28, 1946.
LaTh–HStAW, J. A. Topf & Söhne no. 15, leaf 61r.

bonuses they usually received for the years 1944 and 1945; he
did so "without respect to whether these employees, one of
which was even currently in prison, had participated in the
manufacture of the concentration camp crematoria," according to the charges against him by the Erfurt district court in
a trial in 1953 (in which it was actually a question of not com-
plying with the plan for employees and finances).[4] According
to the court transcript, Wiemokli justified the payments to the
families of the arrested men at the time with the words, "We
didn't want to make the women and children pay for what the

men were being blamed for. . . . We didn't want to do what the Nazis had done with us."[5] The four wives were paid for three years until March 1949 by the company, which had in the meantime become a *volkseigener Betrieb* (state-owned company). The payments were then finally banned by the umbrella trade association, the VVB (Vereinigung Volkseigener Betriebe, or Association of State-Owned Companies).

On May 10, 1947, the company, which still called itself J. A. Topf & Söhne, became the property of the State of Thuringia, ending the sequestration and returning Willy Wiemokli to the position of manager of the company's accounting department. On June 1, 1948, the company was reorganized as a volkseigener Betrieb with the new name of Topfwerke Erfurt, and at the same time it was assigned to NAGEMA, the association of state-owned mechanical engineering companies for manufacturing food, alcohol and tobacco, refrigeration, and the chemical sector.[6]

Designation as a Persecuted Person of the Nazi Regime

In November 1951 Willy Wiemokli's application for status as a Verfolgter des Naziregimes (VdN; Persecuted Person of the Nazi Regime) was approved. He qualified under the guidelines dated February 1950, which also included Mischlinge who had been arrested or in a camp of the Todt Organization due to "racial reasons" in paragraph 1.13.[1] At the close of 1945 he had already been certified as an *Opfer des Faschismus* (victim of fascism).[2] The VdN district office made a corresponding recommendation for VdN status to the Thuringian state ministry of economic affairs and labor. The VdN certification was based on Wiemokli's imprisonment in Buchenwald and in the forced-labor camp in Suhl.[3] In addition to the moral recognition of wrongs suffered there was a special pension and preferential treatment in assignment of housing and other welfare benefits attached to the status as a VdN. Also certified as VdN were Friedrich Schiller and Heinrich Messing in recognition of their time in prison during the National Socialist regime, which was in fact eleven weeks fewer than the legally required minimum period of six months in the case of Heinrich Messing. These three names can be found today on the memorial for the victims of fascism dedicated in 1984 in the main Erfurt cemetery, with Willy Wyjmoklyj's name in the original spelling.[4]

Investigation of Company Management

Even in the state-owned company, Willy Wiemokli's professional knowledge was valued. In 1950 he was promoted to chief accountant and thus was responsible for the financial affairs of the entire company.[1] For October 1949 we have evidence that Wiemokli had been active on the management board of the SED companies group. Even now there was to be no peace and quiet in his life. On November 24, 1950, four managing employees were arrested again, this time by the *Volkspolizei* (people's police): Herbert Bartels, who had become director under Wiemokli as the sequestrator; the longtime company's sales *Prokurist* Max Machemehl; the senior engineer Paul Erdmann, who together with his colleague Fritz Sander had signed business correspondence with the SS; and the sales clerk Wilhelm Gleitz. The charge read, "crimes against humanity under Allied Control Council Law no. 10." This law of December 20, 1945, provided for the "punishment of persons guilty of war crimes, crimes against peace and against humanity." The four men were fired without notice. What could have triggered these arrests, according to the Erfurt chief state prosecutor, might have been a notification in the summer of

57

1950 from the SED companies group to the SED district office about files having been burned in the office. There was the
concern that those in charge who had participated in business
with the SS before 1945 had wanted to make evidence disap-
pear. The destruction of files was in itself harmless; however,
in the search of the offices after the arrests evidence of complicity was found—for example, in the case of Paul Erdmann.
Had Wiemokli as a member of the SED companies group finally seen his last chance to bring to account those working for
the company who had participated in crimes—even if he had
worked closely with these men for years? It is rather improbable, but there's no way now to trace his role in these arrests.
The investigation was closed in February 1951. The chief state
prosecutor said his decision was based on the fact that there
was no criminal offense found. From the files it can be seen
that the investigation was closed under the pressure of the Soviet Control Commission, which had replaced the Soviet military administration as of October 10, 1949. The four men were
released from arrest on February 23, 1951, but nevertheless did
not return to work at the company.[2]

As a result of the arrests Harry Dörr, a licensed engineer
for aviation technology, twenty-nine years old at the time, was
hired as works manager in November 1950. He was the technical director and had only been employed for a few weeks.
By 1952 Dörr's management had led to a massive drop in production, which initially was due to lack of orders and—after
the spring orders came in—was mainly due to lack of raw
materials. In the planned economy, obtaining raw materials
was the responsibility of the ministry for mechanical engineering; however, reparations and export to the Soviet Union
took priority. With the raw materials promised him but never

delivered, Dörr had hoped to make up the gap in the production plan by the summer of 1952, and therefore he had not reduced the number of workers even though he had no work for them. Chief accountant Wiemokli had already told Dörr in April 1952 about the company having too many workers, but Dörr paid no attention. At the end of June 1952 Willy Wiemokli resigned as chief accountant "for health reasons and because I really cannot get things done," as he later testified.[3] Only at the beginning of September 1952 were a hundred workers laid off from the company, which had been renamed on April 30 NAGEMA VEB Machine Works Nikos Belojannis Erfurt.[4]

Imprisonment Again for Wiemokli

On September 24, 1952, works manager Dörr was arrested, and four months later, on January 31, 1953, his former chief accountant Wiemokli was also arrested. In February 1953 Harry Dörr and Willy Wiemokli were charged in the Erfurt district court (today the Thuringian state court) with "failure to fulfill the production quota and failure to comply with employment and financial plans." The legal basis for trial was Order no. 160 of SMAD, issued December 3, 1945, which punished acts of economic sabotage and carried a maximum penalty of death. After a three-day trial, February 16–18, 1953, Dörr was sentenced to six years in prison and Wiemokli to three. Both had been previously fired by the company. In the sentencing opinion of the court as well as in the report of the trial in the newspaper *Das Volk* on February 27, 1953, it becomes clear that this was a sort of show trial whose point was to impress the public.[1] The harshness of the sentence can only be understood in the context of the economic and political developments in the very new German Democratic Republic. In the summer of 1952 the SED leadership had announced a "planned development of socialism" in cooperation with the Soviets. The increase in defense expenditures, the emphasis on heavy industry, and the repression of independent farmers and artisans had a negative effect on the economy and the results of the policy were unpopular. In this tense situation the SED leadership sought scapegoats among those in management. Thus the bad decisions of management of VEB Machine Works Nikos Belojannis were now portrayed as "damaging the people's property," the "basis of our economy," and "development of socialism," which, the court wrote, "as a matter of principle earns a prison sentence."[2]

In the case of Harry Dörr one can say with certainty that the sentence was not justified, his mismanagement drawing a punishment of six years in prison. This is just as true for Willy Wiemokli, but in his case there are other questions. Why was he the only one from the company's management who was prosecuted—when he had already resigned his position as chief accountant in the summer of 1952? In the seventeen-page judgment by the Second Criminal Division of the District Court of Erfurt, which set forth the basis of the sentence, it was pointed out several times that Wiemokli had demanded a reduction in the number of workers earlier. The charges that Wiemokli had "neither told the defendant Dörr in writing of the legal violation of orders about the excess wages and salaries," nor "refused to make these payments in violation of the plan and therefore illegal," were all refuted in detail by Wiemokli's attorney.[3]

There are indications that Willy Wyjmoklyj's arrest and sentence were connected to his Jewish origin. Part of the Stalinist policy of repression at the time by the GDR ruling party, the SED, was both the fight against the Protestant church as well as the repression of Holocaust survivors, which reached a high point at the beginning of 1953 and included house searches in the Jewish community as well as arrests of

Jewish Communists. With this policy the SED was following that of Stalin, who wanted to use the latent anti-Semitism in Eastern Europe to consolidate his power and simultaneously eradicate potential internal party opposition. What is known as the Slánsky trial in Prague at the end of November 1952 sent a signal to the entire Soviet Empire. Rudolf Slánsky, born in 1901, had been a Communist since he was twenty years old and was at the time of his trial the general secretary of the Communist Party of Czechoslovakia. As the apparent head of an "anti-state conspiracy ring" he and ten other codefendants were sentenced to death after a show trial and executed. Slánsky and most of the other high-level Communist functionaries were Jews. It is striking that Dörr was arrested two months before and Wiemokli two months after the Slánsky trial. The company's party organization, which until shortly before had been Willy Wiemokli's political home, held a seminar on the Slánsky trial on February 13, 1953, and took a "position in connection with the irresponsible actions of management personnel in our company." "The working class demands," according to the unanimously passed resolution, "that these elements be stopped." The state prosecutor should "punish the guilty parties" from their own company "to the full extent of the law."[4] Therefore, charges against Dörr and Wiemokli were made in the context of Rudolf Slánsky's execution and the two defendants bore the effect of the current political prejudice. The SED, in which Wiemokli had wanted to help in its new anti-fascist beginning, now declared him to be a criminal. Slánsky, it should be noted, was legally rehabilitated posthumously in 1963, and by the Communist Party in 1968.

Wiemokli was not only vulnerable as someone of Jewish origin but at the same time he could be discredited as someone who, despite his own Jewish father's murder, had served the accomplices back then. The payments Wiemokli as the sequestrator had approved to the family members of the four arrested engineers in 1946 were, to be sure, not a part of the criminal charges, but still showed up in the sentencing opinion in connection with the detailed description of the defendant Wyjmoklyj. His draconian sentence thus also took on an anti-fascist hue.[5] At the same time his "bad experiences from the Nazi period and . . . some conditions of ill health" were asserted as the basis of "mitigating" his sentence. Otherwise the "punishment would have been more serious."[6] Willy Wyjmoklyj spent his eighteen days of detention awaiting trial, counted as part of his prison sentence, incarcerated in the same prison on Andreasstrasse where his father had been sentenced. Father and son both had to bear the costs of their trials.[7]

On the basis of the newspaper report in *Das Volk*, the district office of the Erfurt VdN, which was still headed by Fahrland, the same president as when Wiemokli had been certified as a VdN in 1951, now suggested that Willy Wiemokli should be stripped of his status as a Persecuted Person of the Nazi Regime under paragraph 5c of the guidelines dated February 10, 1950 (committing a "reprehensible, punishable act").[8] On June 16, 1953, it became official, one day before the workers' uprising on June 17, 1953. The party leadership itself had triggered the uprising when they increased the work quotas in the state-owned enterprises in May 1953, thus turning even the workers into opponents.

Rehabilitation

Already before, and more so after the uprising was crushed by Soviet tanks, the SED leadership had distanced itself from implementing a Soviet directive to "force the implementation of socialism." To do this the ministers' council of the GDR had even decided on June 11, 1953, to review arrests, criminal trials, and sentences for supposed economic crimes. Faced with this development the VdN office, still under Fahrland as president, demanded a "favorable consideration for dismissal" on August 5, 1953, and referred to the "most serious persecution," that "Comrade Wiemokli . . . and his family had been exposed to during the Nazi regime." Fahrland now suddenly understood that "the health of Comrade Wiemokli . . . would be completely jeopardized by the rather long prison stay," and it had to be considered "with his mental health" that "he was emotionally in danger."[1] On September 10, 1953, the VdN Social Commission withdrew "its application to invalidate the status of Comrade Wiemokli." The request was supported by the company's party organization of the SED, which just nine months earlier had called for punishment "to the full extent of the law." On July 22, at the request of his wife, Erika, all the residents of the building at Gustav-Adolf-Strasse 2a joined in to urge that Willy Wyjmoklyj be amnestied.[2]

The petition for clemency was granted and Willy Wiemokli was released from prison on October 23, 1953, almost nine months after he had been sentenced. He was imprisoned in the GDR longer than he had been under National Socialism. His sentence was immediately suspended. On November 10, 1953, Wiemokli had his status as a Persecuted Person of the Nazi Regime restored. His new VdN identity card was back-dated to June 16, 1953, which is the date that his VdN status had been invalidated.[3]

The remainder of his sentence was only finally dismissed on March 28, 1956. On July 27, 1957, the attorney general of the GDR vacated the judgment of February 1953 so that Wiemokli no longer was considered as having a criminal record.[4] After his release from prison, Willy Wiemokli, who had been dismissed from the VEB Machine Works Nikos Belojan-nis when he was arrested, did not return again to "his" factory. For health reasons, he could no longer manage a full-time job; even before his arrest his capacity for work had been reduced by 40 percent.[5]

His wife, who, according to her own statement, was "only a housewife" in the first years after the war, had taken a posi-tion again as a bookkeeper at the same time her husband was released in October 1953. Her husband, of course, no longer had a source of income. In 1954 she resigned her position again to take care of her husband—as she wrote in her curriculum vitae.[6] Willy Wiemokli was then forty-five years old. In 1956 he was working again in the town of Gotha, twenty-five kilo-meters away. A police certificate of good conduct states that he was an amiable, pleasant neighbor according to his house-mates, who would be "positive in political respect"; that is, he displayed no critical opinions of the state.[7]

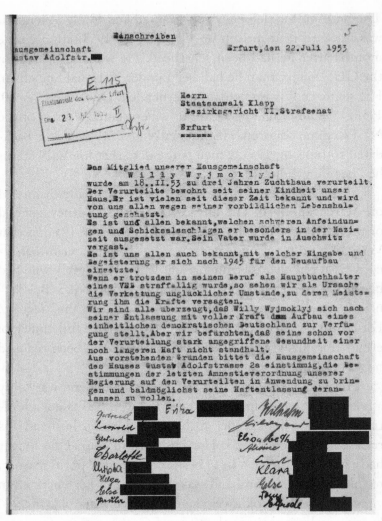

Einschreiben

...ausgemeinschaft
...stav Adolfstr.▪

Erfurt,den 22.Juli 1953

Herrn
Staatsanwalt Klapp
Bezirksgericht II.Strafsenat

Erfurt
═════

Das Mitglied unserer Hausgemeinschaft
    W i l l y   W y j m o k l y j
wurde am 18..II.53 zu drei Jahren Zuchthaus verurteilt.
Der Verurteilte bewohnt seit seiner Kindheit unser
Haus.Er ist vielen seit dieser Zeit bekannt und wird
von uns allen wegen seiner vorbildlichen Lebenshal=
tung geschätzt.
Es ist und allen bekannt,welchen schweren Anfeindun=
gen und Schicksalsschlägen er besonders in der Nazi=
zeit ausgesetzt war.Sein Vater wurde in Auschwitz
vergast.
Es ist uns allen auch bekannt,mit welcher Hingabe und
Begeisterung er sich nach 1945 für den Neuaufbau
einsetzte.
Wenn er trotzdem in seinem Beruf als Hauptbuchhalter
eines VEB straffällig wurde,so sehen wir als Ursache
die Verkettung unglücklicher Umstände,zu deren Meiste=
rung ihm die Kräfte versagten.
Wir sind alle überzeugt,daß Willy Wyjmoklyj sich nach
seiner Entlassung mit voller Kraft dem Aufbau eines
einheitlichen demokratischen Deutschland zur Verfü=
gung stellt.Aber wir befürchten,daß seine schon vor
der Verurteilung stark angegriffene Gesundheit einer
noch längeren Haft nicht standhält.
Aus vorstehenden Gründen bittet die Hausgemeinschaft
des Hauses Gustav Adolfstrasse 2a einstimmig,die Be=
stimmungen der letzten Amnestieverordnung unserer
Regierung auf den Verurteilten in Anwendung zu brin=
gen und baldmöglichst seine Haftentlassung veran=
lassen zu wollen.

12. Letter from the residents of the apartment house at Gustav-Adolf-Strasse 2a for Willy Wyjmoklyj to State Prosecutor Klapp, July 22, 1953. The signature in the center above the others is that of his wife. Most of the eighteen who signed the letter are

(continued on facing page)

women. The family names have been redacted by the archive for privacy reasons. LaTh–HStAW, Bezirksstaatsanwaltschaft Erfurt (Regional state prosecutor's office Erfurt) no. 1213/2, leaf 5r.

A member of our apartment house, Willy Wyjmoklyj, was sentenced to three years in prison on February 18, 1953. The person convicted has been living in our apartment building since his childhood. Many have known him since then and he is esteemed by all of us because of his exemplary conduct.

We all know what bitter hostility and blows of fate he endured during the Nazi years. His father was gassed in Auschwitz.

We also all know how he dedicated himself with enthusiasm to rebuilding anew after 1945.

If nonetheless he became a criminal in his work as chief accountant of a state-owned enterprise, we see the reason as the result of unfortunate circumstances that he did not have the power to master.

We are all convinced that after he is released Willy Wyjmoklyj will make himself available for rebuilding a united, democratic Germany with all his strength. We fear, however, that his health, already greatly compromised before he was sentenced, will not stand a still longer imprisonment.

For these reasons the residents of the apartment house at Gustav Adolfstrasse 2a unanimously request that the provisions of the last amnesty ordinance of our government be applied to the man convicted and to allow his release as soon as possible.

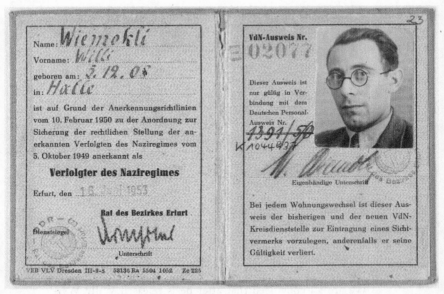

13. VdN identity card of Willi Wiemokli, backdated to June 16, 1953. LaTh–HStAW, Bezirkstag und Rat des Bezirkes Erfurt (District Assembly and Council of the District of Erfurt), VdN no. 3513, leaf 22av–23r.

As she did under the persecution during the National Socialist regime, Erika remained loyal to Willy. Even when the sentence handed down on her husband was a "terrible blow," which had "shattered her to the core," she continued to be loyal to the GDR regime and even volunteered in the city senate of Erfurt.[8]

In 1975 Willy Wiemokli, who was living in the apartment where his parents had lived at Gustav-Adolf-Strasse 2a with his wife, Erika, asked the District VdN Commission for a new apartment because the "issue of heating, carrying coal and ashes to and from the fourth floor . . . was becoming more and more difficult."[9] The couple was assigned an apartment at Pragerstrasse 11/87. Willy Wiemokli died on December 11, 1983, shortly after his seventy-fifth birthday. His wife survived him by six years. Thanks to the renewed designation as a Persecuted Person of the Nazi Regime, she received a monthly pension for survivors of a VdN designee until her death.[10]

Concluding Comments

It is not easy to come to a final conclusion about what Willy Wiemokli experienced and what he did. The words of Willy Wiemokli that we are certain he said all come from official files, having an official purpose. What he thought and felt remains unknown to us.

As early as 1934, the Jewish author Arnold Zweig defined the tragedy of the half Jew in the following words:

> When the pathological savagery of Hitler's followers went about translating the program of their Führer into reality, they took possession of the innermost, deepest part of the soul of the class of humans who were born of a marriage of a Jewish and non-Jewish spouse with a brutality they even boast of now, and with the imagination of goons. . . . Before barbarism burst forth, the marriage of one's parents, one's relationship to father or mother were for these humans a carefully protected quantum of private life. . . . And now the Nazi's hand suddenly stretches forth to flip through the marriage register and tags the children of such marriages in order to cut them off from the majority of their fellow citizens. The tag assigns them to a minority, which only in the rarest cases do they know of and have no knowledge of as a result of their upbringing, and they are made outcasts.

Their very sense of self must be shocking because their very sense of self has been shattered.[1]

Willy Wiemokli was a profoundly loyal and dutiful person toward other people who were close to him personally, especially his parents. His mother, Anna, had been an example of loyalty; as a non-Jewish woman she had been put under great pressure to divorce, a choice that would have immediately exposed her husband, David, considered to be Jewish, to the National Socialist machinery of persecution. Willy Wiemokli was given the same loyalty by his non-Jewish girlfriend, Erika. He supported his father with money, and certainly psychologically as well. It was a great tragedy in his life that he lost his job after he was imprisoned in Buchenwald on account of his father, who was persecuted for being Jewish; as a result he landed at Topf & Söhne in January 1939. Willy Wiemokli was also loyal to people he knew from work when he received support or was needed and could even help. Willy Wiemokli was a good, decent, and ambitious salesman. Throughout his life he was drawn by the fully understandable desire, unattainable for a long time, to be recognized in his work, to be a part of society, and to be able to have an effect. It was loyalty, but also possibly satisfying that he who had been the pariah at work during the National Socialist regime, rose to become the sequestrator, now the most powerful man. Here too in this function, he wanted to fulfill his duty as he understood it: paying out the premiums independent of whether the executives had concluded business with the concentration camps and helping the family members of the engineers who had been arrested.

In 1949 he wrote in his curriculum vitae, "In 1938 my father and I were taken to the KZ Buchenwald as my father was a

Jew and I was a Jewish Mischling." It is the fate of persecution shared with his father that he mentions to justify his status as a Victim of Fascism. But could it be that the adoption of the categories of the National Socialist perpetrators is also evidence of an inability to distance himself from the social milieu that he wanted to be a part of? It was this milieu that first made the Protestant David Wiemokli under National Socialism into a "Jew" and Willy into a "Jewish Mischling."

That after the war Willy Wiemokli took his place as a member of the shop committee and the SED beside those who were accomplices and accessories suited his desire to take on responsibility, and it was probably his personal way of coming to terms with the National Socialist regime. "I immediately . . . returned to work at my last company. I was elected into the shop committee and later appointed the sequestrator of the machine works of Topf & Söhne," he wrote in his curriculum vitae in 1949. A handwritten note below the curriculum vitae reading, "at Topf and Söhne the ovens for the crematoria in the KZ camps were manufactured," is a clue that he had been personally confronted with this charge.[2] He had to have understood the company's complicity in the National Socialists' crimes. After all these losses, however, which the National Socialists had inflicted on him, he probably could not cope with the loss of a home that a position in the company meant to him. This home was finally taken from him against his will by the German Democratic Republic. From a moral perspective Wiemokli was an accessory, but not an accomplice, even when he was working on the orders from the concentration camps in the company's accounting office. He was a victim and at the same time he involuntarily served to exonerate those involved at Topf & Söhne who had, unlike him, the ability to freely decide. Thus after the war he served in a way as proof for Ernst Wolfgang Topf's claim that the company's management had protected "persecuted Jewish fellow citizens and colleagues as much as possible during the National Socialist regime."[3] As a result, Wiemokli was enabling those who had been accomplices and accessories of the Nazi regime who were still in their jobs after 1945, to see themselves as the standard-bearers of a new anti-fascist beginning.

Beate Meyer has comprehensively researched the experience of Jewish Mischlinge and captured their oral history in interviews in Hamburg with many of those affected. She concludes that these people were always aware of the lurking danger of death and that they were still able, at least to some degree, to belong to the *Volksgemeinschaft* by dint of their own efforts—their strategies to avoid conflict, their readiness to pitch in, their ability to establish contact and communication, but also a "self-imposed obligation to be inconspicuous at work and elsewhere."[4] After the war it was possible for Mischlinge to reintegrate into the mainstream German society provided they kept silent and uttered no reproach of those who were fellow travelers and perpetrators.[5] As we have seen in the account of Willy Wiemokli, this was probably not much different in the Soviet Occupation Zone/German Democratic Republic. The anti-fascist new beginning was elevated to a state policy, unlike the policy of West Germany. Even so, work colleagues and neighbors did not want to hear about their own guilt.

Willy Wiemokli shared the inner tensions of all Mischlinge who were persecuted, caught between watching their relatives being murdered and their own ever-present danger of death on the one hand, and their own hopes and efforts to survive on the other. In addition to this dilemma there was his own personal predicament that he sought and found by chance safety with people and a company that later became the technocrats of annihilation by building the ovens of Auschwitz. The measure of his own sorrows is not visible in his choice of laconic words, but in the fact that he became seriously ill.

Willy Wiemokli became entangled in the merciless machinery of two dictatorships. In National Socialism and the Stalinist German Democratic Republic he tried to become the master of his fate and to remain true to his personal moral code. But he could only fail.

Translator's Afterword

Willy Wiemokli's life is the story of a crushingly ordinary *kleiner Mann* (little guy) who had the misfortune to live in the first two-thirds of the twentieth century. Annegret Schüle and Tobias Sowade wanted to document the life of an almost invisible person, legally a half Jew under the Nuremberg Laws, who was both persecuted under Hitler's race laws and assisted in their implementation.

I chose to translate this book because I felt a visceral surprise on first reading. This silent witness to history was, if anything, a victim of convulsive disruptions in German history. Topf & Söhne not only supplied crematory ovens to the SS—it has also become the name that is emblematic for the entire Holocaust. Looking at this ordinary man doing ordinary work brings the lens so close to the Shoah that our shock almost disappears. Willy Wiemokli's very ordinariness as he worked at the company that manufactured ovens emphasized to me the impossibility of answering the question: how could this catastrophe have happened? A definitive answer remains elusive no matter how granularly the historian sets forth the facts.

Willy Wiemokli's life gives insight into the normalization of accommodating the Shoah. *Between Persecution and Participation* reflects ethnic and long-building national tensions in

Europe, insight into the *mentalité* of modernization, the role of the new engineering elite in a traditional family enterprise, the pervasive and long-term effect of the Nuremberg Laws, postwar continuities, the phantom limb of anti-Semitism, and unanswerable questions about individual choices.

The murder of European Jews is central to understanding how Jews view themselves two and three generations later. Yet, thousands of those sent to die in the concentration camps or rounded up for forced labor did not see themselves as Jews. Willy Wiemokli's biography adds a different dimension to our understanding of what Nazi race policies meant to ordinary Germans. Wiemokli's life, defined as a half Jew after 1935, spans the continuities not just in German history but also German Jewish history beyond 1945 and into the Cold War.

Willy Wiemokli's existence was lost three times. First, there was a self-erasure as his career prospects and employment options narrowed before the war as the Nazi regime increasingly circumscribed his aspirations. Second, there was a trial and a prison sentence for decisions made at the company in the early 1950s. Third, there was exhaustion, which led to early retirement and a relatively early death. At no time is there evidence that Willy Wiemokli connected with the Jewish community before or after the war. Yet both his prewar and postwar travails arise from the imposed identity as a half Jew.

Willy Wiemokli: A Life under Two Dictatorships

Willy Wiemokli had the misfortune of living in Germany during the Third Reich and then in the Soviet-controlled state of the German Democratic Republic. His tragedy is that his father had been born a Jew in Berlin of Polish parents, and under the Nuremberg Laws passed in 1935, he was a Mischling—that is, a person of so-called mixed race, of Jewish and Aryan blood. He didn't embrace Nazi ideology (as far as is known) in any way, and there were certainly Jews who did.[1] But he didn't escape it either. After the war, he did embrace Communism, or at least he joined the Communist Party. But he was still not exempt from anti-Semitism; East German policy stopped short of using the worst historical tropes about Jews as a stand-in for capitalism.

Willy Wiemokli's biography is significant because he was neither a coward nor a hero; his choices were narrow at best. Our current, very American credo of personal responsibility and individual agency fails utterly as a way of comprehending how to evaluate Wiemokli's choices under the Nazi regime and its aftermath, or even whether he had choices.

This very short but exhaustive biography of Willy Wiemokli, written seventy years after the end of World War II, raises questions about what history can tell us. We want to know what happened, of course, but also why it happened, how it happened, and how real people carried it out.[2] Willy Wiemokli's life is a private one—no policy making, no battles, no reflecting on what he heard on the radio or from his neighbors. He was jerked into the history of the Holocaust and of the Cold War. His biography tells us little about what propelled the rise of the Nazis or why the Allies won. An examination of underlying causes is not to be found here.

Willy Wiemokli's life story certainly belongs in the study of history; his biography contributes to the ability of the historian of the Jewish catastrophe, which is still within living memory, to fulfill Leopold von Ranke's dictum that the historian's duty is to tell us "wie es eigentlich gewesen" (how it really was).[3] As I read this brief biography, I was struck by a sense of vertigo worthy of W. G. Sebald's examination of memory's detritus. We have a history of a man who left no trace of himself; yet we have the traces that bureaucrats captured on forms and in documents. If the purpose of the study of history or memory is to retrieve lost linkages, the reader must excavate multiple layers of discontinuous history within one lifetime.

Were it not for the biographers of this little book I have translated, Willy would be another unknown person whose impossible choices could be summed up with "one does what one has to do in order to survive." This response is true enough but is unsatisfactory. Something niggles in the back of the mind. Schüle and Sowade have presented Willy Wiemokli as an individual whose status as a half Jew in the employ of a manufacturer of the ovens raises questions about legality and morality. He may not have been legally responsible in any meaningful sense of the word, but his moral responsibility is, given the circumstances, ambiguous. What do we, the readers, do with that realization?

Willy Wiemokli's postwar life, in which we see more continuities than discontinuities with his life under Hitler, bears witness to the truth of William Faulkner's quip, "History isn't dead. It's not even past." Even with the passage of time, the Holocaust and its immediate aftermath have historians busy examining the who, why, and how of perpetrators and victims. It is not possible to deny or dispute that the Shoah happened.[4] It is possible, as the generations pass, that the Shoah can be forgotten. What are we remembering when we pause at ceremonies of remembrance? Could it be that Willy Wiemokli's biography, of an entirely normal, comprehensible person in an incomprehensible situation, with a moral boundary line less than self-sacrificingly sharp, reverberates now because we know what happens during the sleep of reason?

Identity

Under the imperial rule of Kaiser Wilhelm II and throughout the Weimar Republic, Willy Wiemokli was a German of Jewish ancestry. Legally, and apparently socially, the baptized father and his Lutheran son weren't marginalized outsiders. The rantings in the press about the Jewish threat to German society were not directed at them; they weren't Jewish. Many Germans with a Jewish parent or grandparent, baptized or not, saw themselves as Christian. "Tens of thousands of German Jews were not Jews at all, in their own eyes."[5] They weren't Mischlinge until the Nuremberg Laws made them so in 1935.

To be of Polish Jewish ancestry added another layer to the anti-Semitism and anti-Semitic policies and laws. In the story of what happened to Willy Wiemokli's father we see that no acculturation, assimilation, or baptism sufficed to protect him. Willy Wiemokli's grandfather Nachmann Lejb Wyjmoklyj was a Polish Jew who, along with thousands of other Eastern European Jews (Ostjuden), had made his way to Berlin from the shtetls in Poland. The father David Wyjmoklyj was born in Berlin in 1876. David Wyjmoklyj followed the path of many Ostjuden and their children: he rapidly assimilated, married a Christian, and converted to Lutheranism. It wasn't only Jews from Eastern Europe but German Jews in general who were in increasing numbers "dissolving gradually into the larger culture of Germany. . . . The process of assimilation was accelerating fast, with thirty-five Jewish-Christian marriages for every one hundred Jewish-Jewish marriages in Berlin by the outbreak of the First World War, compared with only nine around 1880, . . . Twenty-thousand German Jews were baptized between 1880 and 1920. In a community numbering little more than half a million, these numbers were significant."[6]

There was no reason for Willy Wiemokli to identify as Jewish before the Nuremberg Laws declared him a half Jew. Willy evidently had no Jewish schooling; he was never a member of a Jewish community. His apprenticeship and first jobs were in fashionable department stores owned by highly successful Jewish merchants. German Christians and German Jews had done business with each other on all levels right up to the Nazi boycotts that started in 1933 and the forced Aryanization of Jewish businesses under the 1938 Verordnung über die Zwangsveräusserung jüdischer Gewerbebetriebe und Geschäfte (Law on Expropriation of Jewish Enterprises and Businesses). Throughout Germany around one hundred thousand Jewish-owned businesses had to be handed over or sold to German Aryans.[7] In Thuringia alone, 650 family businesses were Aryanized.[8] Many Jewish owners fled and, as Monika Gibas writes in *Fates of Jewish Families in Thuringia 1933–1945*, Protestants with Jewish ancestors fled "a poisoned Germany." Gibas includes an account of Walter Spiegel, whose story illustrates that Willy Wiemokli's fate was not unique or atypical. The point of comparison lies not in whether the former was, according to the Nuremberg Laws, a full Jew, and the latter a half Jew. Nor is it a question of whether half Jews were not typically rounded up on Kristallnacht. The point of comparison is that in the tumble of events, the shared fate is the violence directed at the "Jew."

Spiegel, the assimilated Jew, was taken to Buchenwald following the Kristallnacht pogrom. So was Willy Wiemokli, the baptized Lutheran son of a baptized Jew, and so was his father, the assimilated baptized Jewish son of Ostjuden. "Taken to Buchenwald" meant descending from the transports, running through a gantlet of SS men with clubs and iron bars, onto the *Appellplatz* (roll-call grounds), where they stood for hours before finally allowed to sit, but not to move. More than 30,000 Jews were arrested and 26,000 transported to a number of different camps; almost a third, 9,828, were delivered into the *Pogromsonderlager* (pogrom special camp) at Buchenwald. This camp within a camp consisted of five barn-like barracks and was enclosed by barbed wire. Here there were no sleeping quarters as such; no windows, only a dirt floor muddy from winter rain, and no respite from SS beatings. There was only cabbage soup to eat, and several prisoners shared one bowl without a spoon. By February 1939 many were released if they agreed to emigrate and renounce any claim to their property. Those who dallied in emigrating could find themselves rearrested.[9] The Wiemokli father and son, as well as Walter Spiegel, were fortunate. Spiegel was released from Buchenwald only after several weeks, and in January 1939 the family immigrated to Cincinnati, Ohio. Safe, but stripped of his belongings, pension, and savings, Spiegel's experience shows the choice, if one even had a choice, of exile could be a painful uprooting from home.

Victor Klemperer's diaries, *I Will Bear Witness*, could be said to be the record of a baptized German who was stunned by the professional and emotional exile from who he thought he was in German society—an exile forced on him by the various race laws. He was an astute observer of the noose tightening around Jews and those who thought of themselves as Protestant and German as any other Protestant German. The difference between Willy Wiemokli and Victor Klemperer is that the former knew what his company made and where the ovens were installed, whereas the latter recorded rumors and scanned newspaper reports and letters to construe the fate of friends. Klemperer (1881–1960), the son of a Berlin rabbi, married a Protestant and converted to Christianity. In *I Will Bear Witness*, Klemperer remarks with some frequency on his identity as a German yet says "we Jews." "Perhaps we Jews always want to be something else—some Zionists, the others Germans. But what are we really? I do not know. And that, too, is a question to which I shall never get an answer."[10]

Klemperer's reactions are a key to comprehending the fate of what can happen when the Nuremberg Laws shove both the hyperarticulate and the inarticulate into the margins of society. Klemperer muses on the German identity he's lost; Willy is silent. Klemperer wrote on May 30, 1943, "*I* am German and am waiting for the Germans to come back; they have gone to ground somewhere."[11] In contrast to the fact that we have no evidence that Willy Wiemokli, even within the safety of his family, wrestled with his fate as a German classified as a Jew, Klemperer's diary entries are verbose. He expresses confusion and clutches at what he thought was his German identity: "the thought went through my head: I must formulate an essay: Pro Germania, contra Zion from the contemporary standpoint of the German Jew."[12] In his frightful circumstances in the Jews' house, with too little food, call-ups to exhausting labor service shoveling snow that endangered his weak heart, and subject to Gestapo searches that might find his notes on the degradation of the German language he loves for his *Language of the Third Reich*, Klemperer discovers his Jewish identity, or rather that assimilated/unassimilated mixture of German Jewish identity:

> What shakes me in Elbogen's *History of the Jews in Germany*, which I have now plowed through to the end . . . , is the precariousness of my position as a German. Equal rights for Jews not until 1848, restricted once again in the 1850s. Then in the 1870s anti-Semitism already stronger again and, in fact, all of Hitler's theory already developed. I knew very little of all of that—and perhaps did not want to know anything of it. Nevertheless: I *think* German, I *am* German—did I not give it to myself, I cannot tear it out of myself. What is tradition? Everything begins with *myself.* No, certainly with my parents. If in his youth Father had accepted the American rabbinate he was offered.[13]

Neither Willy Wiemokli nor his father bear witness on their newly assigned identity even as to daily difficulties, while Klemperer notes at length his anguished discovery that his baptism did not make him non-Jewish. A Jewish friend "again and again attacks me for the 'comedy' of my baptism," and tries to win him back to "national Jewry," by which he means Zionism.[14] The very phrase *baptized Jew* speaks of a split identity, acknowledged or not. Klemperer sees his identity, split between Jewish and German, mirrored in the novel he is reading, the 1920 novel by Sammy Gronemann, *Tohuwabohu* (Utter Chaos). The novel captures the illusion that was to prove a delusion that a Jew could become a German. "I am fighting the hardest battle for my Germanness now. I must hold on to this: I am German, the others are un-German. I must hold on to this: The spirit is decisive, not blood. I must hold on to this: On my part Zionism would be a comedy—my baptism was *not* a comedy."[15]

The Nuremberg Laws

Within three months of taking power, the Nazis passed the Gesetz zur Wiederherstellung des Berufsbeamtentums (Civil Service Restoration Act) on April 7, 1933. This law excluded so-called non-Aryans from the civil service, which included teachers and university professors. Guidelines were issued on August 8, 1933, to clarify who was a non-Aryan. "Non-Aryans are those who are descended from non-Aryan, that is, Jewish parents or grandparents. It suffices if one parent or one grandparent is non-Aryan." Further, "whoever wishes to qualify for the Reich civil service must prove that he and his spouse are of Aryan descent." Also, "any Reich civil servant who wishes to marry must prove that the person he wishes to marry is of Aryan descent."[16] For the Wiemoklis such laws did not mean dismissal from a job.

In 1935, at the annual party rally in Nuremberg, the Nazis announced new race laws that went into effect on September 15, 1935, to clarify whose blood was Jewish and whose was not, and whose was mixed and to what degree it was mixed. The law against racial mixing was called the Gesetz zum Schutz des deutschen Blutes und der deutschen Ehre (Law for Protection of German Blood and German Honor). Jews were forbidden to marry or have sexual relations with those "of German blood" or employ a female with "German or kindred blood" as domestic servants. The Reichsbürgergesetz (Reich Citizenship Law), which also took effect on September 15, 1935, limited political rights and Reich citizenship to someone of "German or kindred blood." Just a month later, on October 18, 1935, a third statute, the Gesetz zum Schutz der Erbgesundheit des deutschen Volkes (Law for the Protection of Hereditary Health of the German People), listed categories that qualified for sterilization "in the judgment of medical science." None of these laws, however, defined "Jew." By mid-November, the Erste Verordnung zum Reichsbürgergesetz (First Regulation under the Reich Citizenship Law) remedied the deficit. Articles 2 and 5 tried to define a Mischling. Even so, articles 6 and 7 provided loopholes. Article 6 gave the Reich minister of the interior and the Führer's representative the power to determine other requirements for "purity of blood." Article 7 acknowledged these regulations were not absolutely binding: "The Führer and Reich Chancellor can grant exemptions from the regulations laid down in the law."[17]

Neither the law nor the first regulation contained the terms *Mischling ersten Grades* or *zweiten Grades* (a person of mixed blood of the first degree or second degree for a half Jew or quarter Jew). On November 26, 1935, less than two weeks after the first regulation had been issued, Secretary of the Reich Ministry of the Interior Wilhelm Frick banned mixed marriages with the Verbot von Rassenmischehen (Prohibition of Racially Mixed Marriages). Apparently there had been some confusion since "mixed marriage" had been a term used for Christian confessional difference of the bride and groom (e.g., Protestant and Catholic). By 1938 the authorities, using the party's official periodical, *Nationalsozialistische Monatshefte*, reminded everyone that they had intentionally introduced these terms because "political Catholicism" continued to recognize the meaning of Mischehe only in canonical terms; it was therefore *dringend erforderlich* (urgently necessary) to use Mischehe only in the sense of a racially mixed marriage, and not to use the term *Rassenmischehe*.[18]

A certain level of frustration can be seen as the Nazi policy makers struggled to define who was a Jew and what to do with those who had Aryan blood in certain quantities. By March 1942, when the Final Solution was being implemented, Himmler wrote to the head of the SS main office regarding the matter of what to do about Mischlinge: "I urgently request that no decrees should be issued concerning the concept of a Jew. We only tie our hands with all these stupid definitions."[19]

The Nuremberg Laws remained in effect until September 20, 1945, when they were repealed by Allied Control Council Law no. 1 (CCL 1), which voided the Law for the Protection of German Blood and German Honor as well as twenty-four other laws and regulations. Further, in article 2, the Allied order prohibited any discrimination on the basis of race, nationality, creed, or opposition to the National Socialist German Workers' Party or its doctrines.[20]

Fluid Identity

The Nazis wildly overestimated the number of Jews in all official categories—full, half, quarter, or mixed. Further complicating the count was the question of how to count. An early postwar analysis of the German census of May 17, 1939, wherein "Jews" were counted according to the Nuremberg Laws, notes that numbers cited by Nazi propaganda were exaggerated.[21] The Reichsgesundheitsführer (Reich Health Leader) Dr. Leonardo Conti claimed 300,000 "non-Mosaic" Jews, 750,000 Mischlinge, and 500,000 full Jews."[22] Instead of Conti's 1.5

million partially or fully Jewish Germans, the May 1939 census found a total of 318,000. In 1939, according to this postwar analysis, there were 52,005 Mischlinge of the first degree (of whom Willy Wiemokli was one) and 32,669 Mischlinge of the second degree. The concerns of Jewish community leaders today about the children of mixed marriages not identifying as Jewish have historical precedent: Only 10 percent of the children of mixed marriages were raised as Jews in 1939. Earlier, even before 1933 and before the persecution of Jews was codified by the Nuremberg Laws in 1935, a mere 15–25 percent of children of mixed marriages were raised as Jews. By 1939 many Jews from Germany as well as from neighboring countries had emigrated, generally to Palestine or to the United States. At the time there were still twenty-four cities in Germany with more than one thousand Jews—Erfurt was not one of them. The success of the Nuremberg Laws in depriving Jews of their economic basis can be seen by comparing the employment statistics of 1933 (240,487 Jews gainfully employed—or 48.12 percent) with those of 1939 (34,102—or 15.6 percent). In 1939 the remaining 84.4 percent were either unemployed (165,620) or part of the household of the employed (17,766). The employment numbers of Mischlinge of the first degree were slightly better (25,410—or 45 percent). Willy Wiemokli was very fortunate indeed to be employed by Topf & Söhne in 1939. Half Jews were even a little better off than Mischlinge of the second degree (14,177 employed—or 40 percent).

In January 1933 there were slightly more than five hundred thousand Jews in Germany, one-third of whom lived in Berlin. After Jews were dismissed from their jobs because of the 1935 Nuremberg Laws, a refugee crisis developed—many people wished to leave and few countries were willing to

accept them. In July 1938 thirty-two countries, including the
United States, met in Evian, France, and only the tiny Do-
minican Republic agreed to accept more refugees. In October
1941 Jewish emigration was officially forbidden.[23] "On May 1,
1941, there were still 168,972 Jews in Germany and on October 1 . . . deportations began."[24] By the end of December, there
were 30,000 fewer Jews in Germany. On September 1, 1944,
only 14,574 Jews were tallied. Of these, only 227 were either
married to Jews or single; of these 227 Jews, 195 lived in Berlin and 32 lived elsewhere in the Reich. Of the approximately
540,000 full Jews in Germany in 1933 (not yet including David
Wiemokli, who was considered by the Reich a full Jew only
after 1935), only 19,000 full Jews survived the war. Germany
had driven into exile, emigration, suicide, or death 96.4 percent of its Jewish population.

Willy Wiemokli moved to Erfurt when he was twelve years
old. Of course, his family was not part of the Jewish community there nor would the census have counted the Wiemoklis
as Jewish. Willy did encounter a small but flourishing secularized Jewish community with a long history. Erfurt enters
written history in the eighth century. Soon thereafter in the
ninth century, there are records of Jewish inhabitants, and by
the second half of the twelfth century, there is evidence of a
Jewish community—a mikveh (ritual bath), two synagogues, a
cemetery, and a yeshiva. Typical for so much of early modern
Jewish history in Germany, Jews were expelled from Erfurt in
1453, and it wasn't until 1786 that they were once more legally
permitted to engage in business and to temporarily settle. By
the 1820s, the elements necessary for a Jewish community
were again present: a mikveh, a synagogue, and a cemetery.[25]
By the end of the nineteenth century, many of the Jews, who

often first came to Berlin before moving on, were Ostjuden fleeing pogroms. By the early twentieth century, many had converted to Christianity (such as David Wiemokli). By 1933 Erfurt had 831 Jews (0.6 percent of the total population).[26] By 1939 there were 263 Jews.[27] By then, the census would have counted David Wiemokli as a full Jew and Willy as a half Jew.

The Nuremberg Laws were, as to be expected, enforced by the majesty of the law. The results could be bizarre. In a case that went to the Reich Supreme Court the legal issue was whether an act of sex between a Jew and an Aryan (*Rassen-schande*) outside of Germany fell within the purview of the Reich's Nuremberg Laws. A German Jew was convicted of having sex with an Aryan woman; the act had taken place twice in Prague—once in July 1937 and once in May 1938—both times while Czechoslovakia was an independent country. The Jewish man had appealed his case to the Reich Supreme Court, which ruled in February 1940, by which point Czechoslovakia had been incorporated into the Reich, that "the purpose of the Nuremberg decrees would be undermined if they didn't apply to acts committed abroad."[28] Hersch Lauterpacht, the international lawyer who immediately after the war persuaded Chief Counsel Robert H. Jackson to include "crimes against humanity" in the charges at the Nuremberg trials in 1945, included this case in his 1942 *Annual Digest and Reports of Public International Law Cases (1938–1940)*.

The majesty of the law may have had difficulty in defining who was a Jew, but once defined as a Jew in any degree, prohibitions, from the petty to life-altering, constrained every aspect of life. Between Kristallnacht (November 9, 1938) and the outbreak of the World War II (September 1, 1939), 229 decrees were issued. Between September 1, 1939, and the autumn of 1941, when wearing the yellow star became mandatory, 525 additional anti-Jewish decrees were issued, including a prohibition on buying underwear, shoes, and clothing. Even public displays of sympathy toward Jews were banned, punishable by three months in a concentration camp.[29]

The paradox of identifying Jews by bloodlines while protecting Aryan blood came up against a long history in Germany of secularizing, converting, and marrying outside one's faith. In short, some Aryans had (tainted) Jewish blood and some Jews had a portion of (pure and precious) Aryan blood. The difficulty of defining what to do about Mischlinge was more acute in Germany itself than in occupied Eastern Europe, where Lithuanian or Polish blood wasn't of Aryan racial consequence.

The peril of being Jewish or half Jewish meant that those who could sought a protector. Willy Wiemokli found one in Ernst Wolfgang Topf, who gave him a job and interceded for him when the Gestapo held him for possible *Rassenschande*. A more reliable way to find safe haven was to change one's status, from Jewish or part Jewish to Aryan or part Aryan. One applied for an exemption of one's status under article 7 of the First Regulation of the Reich Citizenship Law. A person who wished to avoid a court case could apply for an *Abstammungsbescheid* (certification of descent) from the Reichssippenamt (Reich Office for Genealogy) under the Reich Ministry of the Interior, which was in charge of issuing certificates of race status. It was expensive, required a medical examination, copies of parents' and grandparents' birth and baptismal certificates, often sworn testimony that the Jewish parent wasn't the biological parent, and that the illegitimate parent, who may have long since died or had emigrated or just disappeared, was not Jewish.

Since the object of the exercise was to prove Aryan blood, one acceptable document was proof of blood transfusion. Such was the conviction that a blood transfusion alone could taint an Aryan that in September 1935 a Jewish doctor who had provided his own blood to save an SA man injured in an automobile accident was hauled before an SA tribunal. Because the doctor was a World War I veteran, the tribunal concluded the SA man's Aryan purity had not been compromised.[30]

Many claims were based on sworn statements of extramarital affairs of a parent or even just on the claim that one looked Aryan rather than Jewish. As one so-called expert reported after his examination, "Der Prüfling zeigt keine jüdischen Rassenmerkmale oder Hinweise auf jüdische Beimischung" (The examinee shows no Jewish racial characteristics or indications of Jewish impurity).[31] The characteristics of nose, lips, hair, nail cuticles, etc., came not from propaganda images but from official guidelines issued by the Reichs-und Preussischen Ministerium des Innern (Reich Ministry of the Interior) on April 27, 1936.[32] These Ähnlichkeitsanalysen (similarity analyses) "compared up to 130 body parts [and used] 'anthropological' photographs."[33]

The Reich Office for Genealogy processed more than fifty-two thousand requests during the war, and was still processing claims at the end of the war.[34] Beate Meyer quotes one anthropological expert in Hamburg who examined the applicants as complaining that he had as many as twenty cases per week.[35] By the middle of the war, as half Jews were drafted for labor service, the SS was annoyed, even shocked, at what was obvious perjury by parents who were desperately turning their children into bastards:

> Current reports suggest the conclusion that Jews in increasing numbers have recently been trying to conceal their Jewish ancestry by claiming they are illegitimate. . . . Relevant observations have been made by Prague, which for the territory of the Protectorate makes the general assessment that women of Aryan descent married to Jews or even already divorced from Jews have sworn in court that the children they have borne were not conceived by their Jewish spouses but were conceived in an extra-marital affair with an Aryan. Further, Jewish women married to Jews try to prove that their children are not fathered by their Jewish spouses but by someone who can no longer be found today or by a deceased Aryan.[36]

Article 7 saved many lives. If the bureaucrat in charge was willing to turn a blind eye to obvious forgeries and false affidavits, he could push the applications through, though not without real danger to himself. Such was Hans Calmeyer, who headed the Stelle zur Entscheidung über die Meldepflicht (Department for the Obligation to Register) within the Department of the Interior that was part of German occupiers' General Commissariat for Administration and Justice in The Hague. This department decided *Zweifelsfälle* (doubtful cases). Documentation shows he approved at least 60 percent of the applicants, and he warned those whose applications were turned down so they could go into hiding. He saved the lives of at least three thousand Jews and half Jews. For almost a year and a half after the war, Dutch investigators saw him as a perpetrator who made self-serving claims, and for some he is still a controversial figure. On March 4, 1992, Yad Vashem posthumously bestowed on Calmeyer the honor of Righteous Among the Nations.[37]

The status of half and quarter Jews became more and more precarious. As the war ground to its apocalyptic close, protection by legal exemption proved fragile. The able-bodied were at the front while the war effort needed labor. Half Jews were subject to deportations or, like Willy Wiemokli, sent to forced-labor camps. They were spared the requirement to take on the official additional name of Israel (for men) or Sarah (for women). They were also spared the requirement to wear the yellow star. In a sardonic joke of history, having worn the star had to be confirmed after the war before the Stalinist East German authorities would deem one innocent of Nazi inclinations during the Third Reich.[38]

The Ovens

Topf & Söhne had been constructing ovens for city crematoria since 1914. Cremation as an alternative to burial became possible in modern Europe with Professor Brunetti's experiments in Padua in 1873 and with Friedrich Siemens's technological innovation of a regenerative furnace in 1874 that reduced a corpse to ashes.[39] "Unfortunately," reported the *British Medical Journal* in 1910, "the movement [cremation instead of burial] was initiated and has been carried on by the anti-clerical party, and thus acquired a sectarian significance."[40] Cremation violated both Jewish and Catholic doctrines about bodily redemption. (Reform and Conservative rabbis are now permitted to officiate at a cremation, but the number remains tiny. The Catholic Church banned cremation until 1963.) Nevertheless, a movement had been born. Early advocates stressed the hygienic nature of burning the body. The Cremation Society of England worked hard to answer "the most delicate legal points," as the *British Medical Journal* wrote, having distributed ten thousand pamphlets and "lent magic lantern slides illustrating the working of crematories in lectures; this it is always pleased to do." Cremation was more respectful: multiple bodies could not be "introduced into one yawning hole without the religious service of any church," as pit burials were described in the 1910 report. Cremation was more sanitary: "It was quite a common thing in many [British] cemeteries, after a number of years had elapsed, to take up the bodies and convey them elsewhere and use the ground again." The report quotes Baron Lister, the inventor of antiseptic surgery, who investigated an outbreak of "septic fever" in his wards in the Surgical Hospital of Glasgow in 1870 and found beneath the floor "the uppermost tier of a multitude of coffins, which had been placed there at the time of the cholera epidemic of 1849, the corpses having undergone so little change in the interval that the clothes they had on at the time of their hurried burial were plainly distinguishable." The 1910 report praised "the great strides" in Germany, thanks to the Feuerbestattung Verein (Cremation Society), which had eighty-four branches throughout the German Empire. In 1900 the rate of cremation in Germany was 0.05 percent; by 1934 the rate was almost 9 percent. Today, about one-third of all funeral rites are cremation, but the numbers vary by regions.[41] In the United States, by contrast, the cremation rate is about 38 percent.

When Ludwig Topf, father of Ludwig and Ernst Wolfgang Topf, committed suicide in February 1914, he was cremated in Gotha in the first German crematorium, built in

1878. His funeral was attended by many, including chamber of commerce president Friedrich Benarys, whose Jewish father, Ernst Benarys, had been cremated in 1893 without the presence of a rabbi.

Prussia legalized cremation in 1911. The law was deemed too restrictive by advocates for permitting widespread access to cremation and the highly charged discussion continued, with the progressive parties facing the center and conservative parties in a stalemate. The positions were embedded in larger ideas about church-state relations, treatment of minorities, and political representation.[42] Finally, after the Nazis came to power, the Feuerbestattungsgesetz von 1934 (Cremation Act of 1934) was passed. The law gave burial and cremation equal status and standardized regulations throughout Germany. It was still in effect in some states until recently. The Cremation Act of 1934 set forth restrictions to ensure a respectful disposal of the body, consideration of the family, and a crematorium designed "to uphold the principles of dignity."[43] After the war, Ernst Wolfgang Topf insisted that the presence of Topf & Söhne's ovens in the concentration camps had been necessary solely as hygienic measures. In *Industrie und Holocaust: Topf & Söhne—Die Ofenbauer von Auschwitz*, Annegret Schüle provides overwhelming documentation—visits by company engineers, patent applications, memoranda—that the company not only knew it was providing ovens with illegal specifications but also that it knew that the use of the ovens in the camps did not conform to the law and did not match use in a municipal crematorium.[44] Selling ovens to the SS was not a question of greed. The ovens sold to the SS, installed in Auschwitz and other concentration camps, and maintained per contract barely constituted 2 percent of the company's total revenues.[45] Nor was it coercion. The SS bought ovens from several suppliers, not just Topf & Söhne. The advantage sought by the Topf brothers by joining the Nazi Party the same year the party came to power and the sale of the ovens with maintenance and repair services for the SS illustrate Richard J. Evans's point that it was important to secure patronage of the powerful within the Nazi regime.[46] It was a sales contract by which what was sold, warrantied, maintained, and improved was normalized.

On January 30, 1933, Adolf Hitler became chancellor of Germany. In March 1933 the first concentration camp was established. The prisoners were political opponents, Communists, Social Democrats, and trade unionists. The camp system quickly expanded. Those who died of beatings, disease, or starvation were cremated in nearby municipal crematoria. Buchenwald opened in July 1937. Within two weeks, "before the first person died, the commandant of the camp had made inquiries of nearby Weimar to see whether those who had died in the camp could be cremated in the city crematorium," and received a positive answer.[47] This meant that outsiders learned of the camps. Very quickly, there were far more corpses than the local crematoria in Weimar, Jena, and Leipzig could handle. The stench of the bodies awaiting cremation also alerted people who lived nearby. The first Topf & Söhne cremation ovens were mobile, oil-heated, and had one muffle or chamber. The design was based on a garbage incinerator designed by the Topf & Söhne engineer Kurt Prüfer in the 1920s.[48] That responsible people at the company knew that the mobile crematoria were intended for the liquidation of entire communities in Poland is in the documents showing that Topf & Söhne calculated capacity.[49] Mobile crematoria did not suffice to burn the dead. Buchenwald had its first crematorium with a double muffle installed by July 1940.

The ovens as used in the camps violated the Cremation Act of 1934, but at first the charade of legality was carefully observed. Topf & Söhne also furnished the legally required urn plaques and ash capsules, which were filled with ashes from multiple bodies. Himmler had decreed in 1940 the ashes of the cremated person had to be in its individual container, as per the law. By 1943 the practice was stopped by a counterdecree—the need to pretend that burial rites were being handled legally was apparently no longer necessary.[50]

The products of Topf & Söhne used in the concentration camps were the factory equipment for industrialized murder and disposal of the murdered. The goal of the engineers at Topf & Söhne was efficiency. Kurt Prüfer added muffles to increase speed and thoroughness to the process of reducing a human body to ashes. Topf manager Fritz Sander testified after the war that in response to his question Prüfer had told him why there were so many corpses in the camps. Prüfer's reply was that people were killed in gas chambers and their bodies burned in crematoria. Taking Prüfer's explanation as a statement of an engineering problem, the sixty-six-year-old Sander designed a superoven and applied for a patent captioned "Continuous-Operation Incineration Oven for Mass Use."[51] Submitted on October 26, 1942, the patent drawing shows a four-story tower with what looks like a macabre version of a water park slide. The patent was never granted during the Third Reich. It was listed in the inventory dated November 26, 1946, of pending patents, including Prüfer's double-muffle incineration oven patented in 1939, used in the death camps.[52]

Knowledge about the equipment Topf & Söhne produced was not secret, but details of its use were not common company knowledge, as Sander's question to Prüfer shows. As to what Willy Wiemokli knew, the only written document we have is his review of Prüfer's invoices.

In 1947 Ernst Wolfgang Topf reestablished J. A. Topf & Söhne in Wiesbaden, located in the American Zone. In 1953 the West German patent office issued a patent (No. 867,731) for an oven, now called *Verfahren und Vorrichtung zur Verbrennung von Leichen, Kadavern und Teilen Davon* (process and apparatus for incineration of carcasses, cadavers, and parts thereof).[53] The 1953 patent, which dealt with technical aspects of incineration with hot air, was not the Sander invention, but was seen as the basis of the company's fresh start in the West.[54] This hit a raw nerve. The 1953 patent was seen as Fritz Sander's invention of 1942. When the historian Gerald Fleming quoted in an op-ed in the *New York Times* on July 18, 1993, Fritz Sander's testimony from discovered records of the 1946 Red Army interrogations of Topf & Söhne employees, a reader responded with the statement that "Topf did eventually receive the patent it coveted for the crematoriums the company had supplied to the Nazis."[55] The patented invention inspired the play *Patent Pending* by the Dutch-born Israeli playwright Wim van Leer, which premiered in London in June 1965. Sander's patent drawing and his testimony of March 7, 1946, to his Soviet interrogators also inspired an art installation by the German-Uruguayan conceptual artist Luis Camnitzer called *Patentanmeldung* (Patent Application). The work was first shown at the Galerie Basta in Hamburg in 1996. In the simple glass tabletop is etched Sander's architectural sketch from the 1942 application, and around the edge on top of the table is a quotation from Sander's testimony. Camnitzer's artistic goal is to present an invention, even one as ghoulish as this, as a creative act unrecognized by a validating review (the Reich patent office in 1942).[56] Camnitzer's table makes the point that Sander was a creative engineer who was incapable of seeing the moral gap between his creation and its purpose.

The Question of Corporate Criminality

The two principals of Topf & Söhne—namely, the brothers Ludwig and Ernst Wolfgang Topf—were subjected to investigation after the war but neither was brought to trial. The US Army arrested Kurt Prüfer on May 30, 1945. Ludwig Topf reacted to the news that he would be arrested by committing suicide on May 31. Prüfer was released two weeks later. Ernst Wolfgang Topf left for Stuttgart, in the American Zone, at the end of June to file for the insurance on his brother's death. Before he could return to Erfurt, the Soviets had taken over control of territory from the Americans in the Soviet Zone, and Ernst Wolfgang was refused permission to return. At the beginning of March 1946 the company, now under Soviet sequestration, received a large order from the Soviet military authorities for brewing and malting equipment and, a few days later, Prüfer, Sander, and two others were arrested. Prüfer was interrogated and he disappeared into the Gulag. In *Industrie und Holocaust* Annegret Schüle meticulously follows the archival trail of the thwarted, dropped, and botched investigations into the criminal responsibility of Ernst Wolfgang Topf. Until his death in 1979, Ernst Wolfgang Topf saw himself as a persecuted victim. East Germany awarded his Communist engineer Heinrich Messing, whose time sheet shows he was working on the ventilation in the disrobing room and gas chamber of Crematorium II from March 8 to 14, 1943, the status of a VdN (Persecuted Person of the Nazi Regime)[57] after the war, and he too is honored in the same memorial grove as Willy Wiemokli.[58]

In the Nuremberg trials, corporations were prosecuted. Directors and managers from I. G. Farben, Hoechst, Flick, Krupp, Ford Werke, and others were investigated, charged, and tried before the International Military Tribunal. I. G. Farben, for example, saw twenty-four defendants in the dock; only thirteen were found guilty; sentences ranged from eighteen months to eight years. Krupp saw fourteen defendants in the dock; one was acquitted, and Alfred Krupp von Bohlen und Halbach was sentenced to ten years and released after serving three. Even though no one from Topf & Söhne came to trial immediately after the war or later in West Germany, a 2012 case study of the company lays out the motivations of ideology, greed, opportunity, competition, fear of state reprisals for failure to cooperate, the culture of perfecting a technology, and the inability to see actions or products in a moral context.[59]

Where legality was a necessary constraint on the creativity of the engineers, Prüfer emphasized that the ovens on offer with new innovations "fulfill[ed] the wishes of legislators" in the Cremation Act of 1934 in his sales pitch for the newest model of ovens sold to the city crematorium of Arnstadt in 1940.[60] Where legality was of no concern and engineering possibilities were unmoored from any moral sensibility, Fritz Sander could write a six-page memorandum dated September 14, 1942, to the company management about the advantages of his continuous-operation incineration oven for mass use:

"I am completely aware that such an oven is to be considered purely as a device of complete destruction, and therefore that all notions of piety, separation of ashes and any traces of emotions must be completely eliminated."[61] The company took note of Sander's letter and requested a sketch of the proposed new oven.

The authors of the 2012 case study, Annika van Baar and Wim Huisman, consider the concept of "state-corporate crime," in which the "symbiosis between states and corporations is usually fluid, complex, and fluctuating."[62] But the Topf case, the authors suggest, presents a different relationship between state and corporation: the corporation facilitates the crime and even provides the means to carry out the state crime more effectively. The death camps, as opposed to the concentration camps and forced-labor camps, became a central image of the Holocaust only after the war when "the political and legal criminalization of what was later called the Holocaust came into existence . . . , for instance by the Nuremberg Trials."[63] There were massacres before the death camps and since—but, as Hannah Arendt remarked, the "fabrication of corpses" was unique.[64] The engineered deaths were made possible by administrative and technical efficiency. "Even today, corporations complicit in international crimes like Topf & Söhne cannot be adjudicated by the court set up to end impunity, the International Criminal Court."[65]

Postwar Response to the Nazi Past

After World War II, there were few Jews in the Soviet Zone, about 4,500.[66] There were 21,454 Jews remaining in all of Germany from less than 600,000 before 1933. These figures do not take into account those in displaced-person camps administered by the United Nations Relief and Rehabilitation Administration.[67] More former German Jews returned to East Germany than to West Germany because "many were convinced that their chance to contribute to a 'better Germany' was in the eastern part," especially if they had been secular and Socialist or Communist.[68] Willy Wiemokli's biographers see his return immediately upon his release from the labor camp, as the Americans swept into Thuringia, to take up his position as accountant at Topf & Söhne as an act of faith that he could contribute to a better Germany. The East German narrative of historical memory—namely, that the victims of the Nazis had not been Jews as such but anti-fascists—promised an identity as someone who now shared his country's fate rather than an identity as a half Jew, whose father had died in Auschwitz. The difference is an identity of being where one belongs as opposed to an identity of finding refuge.

Willy Wiemokli was thirty-seven years old in 1945. He lived another thirty-eight years in Communist-ruled East Germany. The historian Jeffrey Herf remarks that the Nuremberg trials (October 1945–October 1946) were well reported in the newspapers published under Allied occupation in all zones. "The Soviet-run press published full and prominent accounts of the indictments, testimony, evidence, and verdicts." The Nazis' crimes and the details of the death camps were public knowledge. Yet "silence or marginalization, not denial, became the dominant mode of avoiding an uncomfortable past."[69] Willy Wiemokli's Jewish identity, courtesy of the Nuremberg Laws, continued to affect his postwar life. The so-called Jewish question was one of the multiple continuities after 1945 in both East and West Germany as politicians in both countries addressed the immediate past in different but coherent ways.[70]

Herf argues that there were three basic choices for German politicians: (1) impose a dictatorship on a politically unreliable population (the Communists in East Germany); (2) limit engagement with the Nazi past and turn to integrate with the West (conservative Christian Democrat Adenauer in West Germany); or (3) build a postwar democracy through public discussion of the past (liberal Social Democrats Theodor Heuss, Kurt Schumacher, and Ernst Reuter in West Germany).[71]

The construction of public memory of the Nazi past in East Germany followed a different path from the one of silence in the Adenauer restoration in West Germany, but here too the Jewish catastrophe was omitted.[72] The view of the past, seen through the dominant Stalinist filter, was framed as Nazi aggression against Communists. By the time Willy Wiemokli was arrested and sentenced for economic sabotage, Jews were no longer victims of Nazi persecution but dangerous and subversive agents. Stalinist East German government turned on Communist activists who had advocated for Jews, using tropes having "a long history in German and European anti-Semitism."[73] The party members who had advocated for restitution to Jews were purged. Restitution, the hardliners said, would only benefit Jews and fascists. As small as it was, the Jewish community was caught up in the purge. Members, including the leader of the Erfurt Jewish community, fled to the West. The purge and flight made headlines in the *New York Times*, such as it did on February 8, 1953: "Jewish Fugitives Reveal Pressures by East Germans: Eight Leaders Say They Were Asked to Back Slánsky Case and Denounce Zionism."

Altogether, 550 of the 2,600 members of the East German Jewish community fled to the West, and the homes of almost all Jews were searched.[74] Herf sees this purge as the turning point for Jews in East Germany; there was no more discussion of Jewish matters. Willy Wiemokli, as his biographers describe, was singled out for harsher treatment in the trial for economic sabotage in 1953 because he was perceived as Jewish.

In 1947 the Department of Labor and Social Welfare in the Soviet Zone published guidelines for issuing identity cards for "Fighters against Fascism" and "Victims of Fascism."[75] There was no restitution or reparations for Jews who had had property destroyed, seized, or stolen by the Nazis. Herf notes that the guidelines did not mention "Jews," but "victims of the Nuremberg racial laws" and "those who wore the yellow star." In 1948 a law was proposed to compensate those designated as "persecuted persons under the Nazi regime." It met with stiff opposition—Ulbricht, the Stalinist leader of the Communist Party in the Soviet Zone, was suspicious of what he saw as the prominence of the question of Jewish compensation. It was "evidence of capitalist restoration."[76] Nevertheless, two days before the German Democratic Republic was founded, on October 7, 1949, the Soviet occupying authorities approved the "Regulation for Securing the Legal Position of Those Recognized as Persecuted by the Nazi Regime." It too distinguished between Communist anti-fascist "fighters" and Jewish "victims." There was no restitution or compensation for lost property, and benefits for housing, health care, and employment were less generous for "victims." The law was approved by the new republic in 1950.[77] For Willy Wiemokli the new law meant that his suffering on account of "race" had not been as much as the suffering of an "anti-fascist" political opponent.

Conclusion

Annegret Schüle and Tobias Sowade have searched the archives for every possible detail about Willy Wiemokli's life. They present the paradox of the non-Jew by birth who is turned into a half Jew by legal fiat. Despite the lack of personal records of any sort, Schüle and Sowade conclude that the traces they find in the archives tell the story of the basic human need for belonging and human loyalty. Willy Wiemokli was at home in Erfurt's secular (high school) and secularized Jewish (apprenticeship and first jobs) milieus. The Nuremberg Laws affixed "half Jew" to him like stigmata. We know much about the possible effects of the external historical context and almost nothing about internal reactions. The external historical context is, of course, the Third Reich, the Holocaust, and the postwar Stalinist dictatorship in East Germany. But for the fact that Willy Wiemokli, a member of a persecuted group, worked for the oven makers, Topf & Söhne, he led a most conventional life of someone who, as far as we know, neither defended the prewar or postwar regimes nor dissented from them. Nor did he influence or implement policy politically or at his workplace. His biography illustrates that his story is unique and, paradoxically, a common one.

Auschwitz and its crematory ovens were not events outside of history. They were not the result of a *mysterium tremendum* to test belief in God or nation, and therefore they are not beyond the reach of historians. The facts show that the Holocaust was very much a result of human decisions, as Willy Wiemokli's life demonstrates. That story we see is extraordinarily nuanced, and not just for Jews be they observant, secular, or baptized, but also for those turned into Jews by statute.

We have a paradox. Willy Wiemokli's biography is one of many different touchstones of the Jewish experience in Germany. Willy Wiemokli cannot remotely be described as even an unobservant Jew, yet his fate is similar to Imre Kertész, who grew up as an unobservant Jew, realizing that his years in the death camp obliged him to be Jewish: "I accept it, but to a large extent it was imposed on me."[78] Willy's biography is a story about the virus of anti-Semitism that doesn't even need the presence of a Jew to manifest itself and find a victim. If there is a lesson here—and history, unlike theology, does not teach a moral—it is that attention must be paid: Willy Wiemokli's life deserves the attention of historians as well as the rest of us. Uncomfortably, the Final Solution is not just a chronicle of innocent victims and evil perpetrators; it is not a question of those who acted versus those who were acted upon. The record from the archives for Willy Wiemokli blurs these boundaries. Although there were indeed heroes and criminals, Willy Wiemokli's biography is about a person who was neither one nor the other; his life defies the Hollywood typologies of villainous Nazis losing and innocents prevailing. We want a narrative that begins poorly but ends well. Such an arc is immensely satisfying because it signifies to us that what happened has meaning—we're safe. Willy Wiemokli's biography confounds us, however detailed the historical record is, and however understandable the human motives may be.

Selected Bibliography

Ameskamp, Simone. "On Fire: Cremation in Germany, 1870s–1934." PhD diss., Georgetown University, 2006.

Anonymous. "Progress of Cremation." *British Medical Journal* 1, no. 2566 (March 1910): 579–81.

Arendt, Hannah, Interview. "Zur Person: Günter Gaus im Gespräch mit Hannah Arendt" [Profile: Günter Gaus in Conversation with Hannah Arendt], Rundfunk Berlin-Brandenburg, October 28, 1964.

Blau, Bruno. "The Jewish Population of Germany, 1939–1945." *Jewish Social Studies* 12, no. 2 (April 1950): 161–72.

Boaz, Rachel E. "The Search for 'Aryan Blood.' Seroanthropology in Weimar and National Socialist Germany." PhD diss., Kent State University, 2009.

Brocke, Edna. "Jews in the New Germany: What Has Changed?" *European Judaism: A Journal for the New Europe* 27 no. 2 (Autumn 94): 73–78.

Burleigh, Michael, and Wolfgang Wippermann. *The Racial State: Germany 1933–1945.* Cambridge: Cambridge Univ. Press, 1991.

"Dokumente des sogenanten Dritten Reiches für den Zeitraum 1933–1945" [Documents of the So-Called Third Reich for the Period 1933–1945]. documentArchiv.de. http://www.document archiv.de/ns.html.

East Germany Synagogues. "Erfurt—Thuringia." http://www.east germanysynagogues.com/index.php/communities/101-erfurt -thuringia-english.

"Erfurt." Jewish Virtual Library. https://www.jewishvirtuallibrary .org/jsource/judaica/ejud_0002_0006_0_06049.html.

Evans, Richard J. "'Nazi Policy towards 'Half-Jews' and 'Mixed Marriages.'" In *David Irving, Hitler and Holocaust Denial.* Holocaust Denial on Trial, Emory University, https://www.hdot.org /evans/#.

———. *The Third Reich in History and Memory.* New York: Oxford Univ. Press, 2015.

Fleming, Gerald. "Engineers of Death." *New York Times*, July 18, 1993.

Gibas, Monika, ed. *Fates of Jewish Families in Thuringia 1933–1945.* Translated by Julia Palme. Erfurt, Germany: Landeszentrale für politische Bildung Thüringen, 2009.

Gilbert, Martin. *The Holocaust: A History of the Jews of Europe during the Second World War.* New York: Holt, Rinehart, and Winston, 1985.

Greaney, Patrick. "Last Words: Expression and Quotation in the Works of Luis Camnitzer." *Germanic Review* 89 (2014): 94–120.

Herf, Jeffrey. *Divided Memory: The Nazi Past in the Two Germanys.* Cambridge, MA: Harvard Univ. Press, 1997.

"Holocaust Denial on Trial." http://www.hdot.org/en/trial/.

Kandell, Jonathan. "Imre Kertész, Nobel Laureate Who Survived Holocaust, Dies at 86." *New York Times,* March 31, 2016.

Klemperer, Victor. *I Will Bear Witness: A Diary of the Nazi Years, 1933–1941.* Translated by Martin Chalmers. New York: Random House, 1998.

———. *The Lesser Evil: The Diaries of Victor Klemperer 1945–59.* Translated by Martin Chalmers. London: Phoenix, 2004.

"Repealing of Nazi Laws." Allied Control Council's Law no. 1 (CCL 1). https://www.loc.gov/rr/frd/Military_Law/Enactments/Volume-I.pdf.

Lipstadt, Deborah. *Denying the Holocaust: The Growing Assault on Truth and Memory.* New York: Penguin, 1993.

Meyer, Beate. *"Jüdische Mischlinge": Rassenpolitik und Verfolgungserfahrung 1933–1945* ["Jews of Mixed Marriages": Racial Policy and the Experience of Persecution 1933–1945]. Munich and Hamburg: Dölling und Galitz Verlag, 1999.

Noakes, Jeremy, and Geoffrey Pridham, eds. *Documents on Nazism, 1919–1945.* New York: Viking, 1974.

Nussbaum, Laureen. "Shedding Our Stars: How German Lawyer Hans Calmeyer Saved Thousands of Jewish Lives in Occupied Holland (1941–1944)." Unpublished manuscript.

Ostow, Robin. "From the Cold War through the Wende: History, Belonging, and the Self in East German Jewry." *Oral History Review* 21, no. 2 (Winter 1993): 59–72.

Pegelow, Thomas. "Determining 'People of German Blood,' 'Jews' and 'Mischlinge': The Reich Kinship Office and the Competing Discourses and Powers of Nazism, 1941–1943." *Contemporary European History* 15, no. 1 (February 2006): 43–65.

Reiser-Fischer, Angelika. "Die zwielichtige Ehrung des Heinrich Messing" [The Ambiguous Tribute to Heinrich Messing]. *Thüringer Allgemeine*, March 7, 2013.

Rosenbaum, Eli M. "German Company Got Crematorium Patent." *New York Times*, July 27, 1993.

Sands, Philippe. *East West Street: On the Origins of "Genocide" and "Crimes against Humanity."* New York: Knopf, 2016.

Schmitz-Berning, Cornelia. *Vokabular des Nationalsozialismus* [The Vocabulary of National Socialism]. Berlin and New York: Walter de Gryter, 1998.

Schüle, Annegret. *Industrie und Holocaust: Topf & Söhne—Die Ofenbauer von Auschwitz* [Industry and Holocaust: Topf & Söhne—Builders of the Ovens of Auschwitz]. 2nd ed. Göttingen: Wallstein Verlag, 2011.

———. *J. A. Topf & Söhne: Ein Erfurter Familienunternehmen und der Holocaust* [J. A. Topf & Söhne: An Erfurt Family Company and the Holocaust]. Erfurt, Germany: Landeszentral für politische Bildung Thüringen, 2014.

Stargardt, Nicholas. *The German War: A Nation under Arms, 1939–1945*. New York: Basic Books, 2015.

Stein, Harry. *Konzentrationslager Buchenwald 1937–1945: Begleitband zur ständigen historischen Ausstellung* [Concentration Camp Buchenwald 1937–1945: Volume Accompanying the Permanent History Exhibit]. Edited by Gedenkstätte Buchenwald. Göttingen: Wallenstein Verlag, 1999.

110 · Between Persecution and Participation

Topf & Söhne. "A Perfectly Normal Company: The Cremation Act of 1934." http://topfundsoehne.info/cms-www/index.php?id=97 &l=1.

United States Holocaust Memorial Museum. "German Jewish Refugees, 1933–1939." https://www.ushmm.org/wlc/en/article.php ?ModuleId=10005468.

Van Baar, Annika, and Wim Huisman. "The Oven Builders of the Holocaust: A Case Study of Corporate Complicity in International Crimes." *British Journal of Criminology: An International Review of Crime and Society* 52 (2012): 1033–50.

van Pelt, Robert Jan, *The Case for Auschwitz: Evidence from the Irving Trial.* Bloomington: Indiana Univ. Press, 2002.

von Ranke, Leopold. *Geschichten der romanischen und germanischen Völker von 1494 bis 1514* [History of the Latin and Teutonic Nations from 1494 to 1514]. 3rd ed. Leipzig: Verlag von Dunder & Humblot, 1885.

Yad Vashem. "Calmeyer, Hans (1903–1972)." http://db.yadvashem .org/righteous/family.html?language=en&itemId=4042996.

———. "Erfurt, Provinz Sachsen, Deutsches Reich." http://db.yad vashem.org/deportation/place.html?language=de&itemId=54 28439.

Notes

Family and Youth

1. Curriculum vitae of Willy Wiemokli, October 13, 1949, LaTh–HStAW, District Assembly and Council of the District of Erfurt—VdN (Persecuted Person of the Nazi Regime) no. 3513, leaf 15r.

2. Registry Office Halle-Nord, Registry no. 531/1908, Information from City Archive of Halle, per email dated December 2, 2014.

3. *Ahnentafel* (genealogical chart) for David Wyjmoklyj, LaTh–StAG, Magistrate's Court of Erfurt no. 1006, Criminal Case File Wyjmoklyj, David, leaf 5.

4. Jutta Hoschek, *Ausgelöschtes Leben: Juden in Erfurt 1933–1945. Biographische Dokumentation, Landeshauptstadt Erfurt, Stadtverwaltung und das Netzwerk "Jüdisches Leben Erfurt"* [Extinguished Lives: Jews in Erfurt 1933–1945. Biographical Documentation in Capital City Erfurt, City Administration and the Network "Jewish Life Erfurt"] (Jena, Germany: Vopelius, 2013), 488.

5. Hoschek, 488. On David Wyjmoklyj's death certificate from Auschwitz, David's father is noted as Nachman and his mother as Estra, née Wysznewicz (the original Polish spelling of her name), July 30, 1943, ITS, 1.1.2.1/629198.

6. See note 3. The addition of "Poland" after "Meseritz," which was added later to David Wyjmoklyj's *Ahnentafel*, indicates that this was not the Meseritz in today's Poland, lying about sixty kilometers east of Frankfurt/Oder and was Prussian at the time, only becoming part of Poland in 1945. Meseritz in the province of Lublin, on the other hand, once again became

111

part of the Polish state reestablished in 1918 and had been part of Russian territory as a result of the division of Poland.

7. On David Wyjmoklyj's *Ahnentafel*, his mother's birthplace was written in by hand. It can be read as either Łuków or Łukom (250 kilometers west of Warsaw).

8. David Wyjmoklyj's *Ahnentafel*.

9. Entry in the Civil Register of the City of Erfurt for David Wiemokli, StadtA Erfurt 2-136-76.

10. Address book of the city of Erfurt 1922–23, StadtA Erfurt 4-0/VIII-128.

11. Willi Wyjmoklyj's graduation certificate from his high school in Erfurt, September 30, 1925, StadtA Erfurt 1-2/232-4244, leaf 542.

12. Volker Freche and Jürgen Zerull, "Humboldtschule zu Erfurt 1879–2009," *Thüringer Naturbrief* [Thuringia Nature Letter], September 4, 2008, http://www.thueringer-naturbrief.de/index.php?option=com_content&task=view&id=4793&Itemid=187.

13. Curriculum vitae of Willy Wiemokli.

From Wyjmoklyj to Wiemokli (and Back)

1. Entry in the civil register. A foreigner's card file has not been preserved in the city archive. That the city administration of Erfurt completed the civil registry pages for those baptized but still persecuted according to "racist standards" as directed by the Gestapo beginning in October 1938 is reported in Hoschek, *Ausgelöschtes Leben*, 13.

Apprenticeship in the Department Store Römischer Kaiser

1. Ruth and Eberhard Menzel, *Das Erfurter Kaufhaus und sein Jahrhundert: Vom Kaufhaus Römischer Kaiser zum Karstadt Themenhaus 1908–2000* [The Erfurt Department Store and Its Century: From the Department Store Römischer Kaiser to the Karstadt House of Themes 1908–2000] (Erfurt, Germany: Karstadt Department Store, AG, 2000), 18–73.

2. In 1933 the empire of Leonhard Tietz was renamed Kaufhof AG under National Socialist pressure. His brother, Oscar Tietz—financed by the

uncle and godfather of the company, Hermann Tietz (1837–1907)—founded the department store company Hermann Tietz. In 1926 Hermann Tietz & Co., which owned the department stores of Adolf Jandorf (1870–1932), another major Jewish entrepreneur, also took over KaDeWe. During the Nazi period, Hertie was born from the name of Hermann Tietz & Co. (since 1994 Hertie has been a part of Karstadt) because the family owners, who were Jewish, had to be removed. Hertie (from *Her*mann *Tie*tz) was already the retailer's own brand name. See Nils Busch-Petersen, *Oscar Tietz: Von Birnbaum/ Provinz Posen zum Warenhauskönig von Berlin* [Oscar Tietz: From Birnbaum/ Province of Posen to Department Store King of Berlin], 3rd ed. (Berlin: Hentrich & Hentrich, 2013). See also Nils Busch-Petersen, *Leonhard Tietz: Fuhrmannsohn und Warenhauskönig—von der Warthe an den Rhein* [Leonhard Tietz: Carter's Son and Department Store King—From the Warthe to the Rhine] (Berlin: Hentrich & Hentrich, 2014), and Nils Busch-Petersen, *Adolf Jandorf: Vom Volkswarenhaus zum KaDeWe* [Adolf Jandorf: From Popular Department Store to KaDeWe] (Berlin: Hentrich & Hentrich, 2008).

3. Hoschek, *Ausgelöschtes Leben*, 9.

4. On the contents of the personnel files, see Menzel, *Kaufhaus*, 58–73. Ruth and Eberhard Menzel cite incorrectly the archive of the city of Erfurt as the location of the files. They are in fact supposed to have always been in the possession of Karstadt, and the Menzels could have viewed them before Karstadt destroyed them after 2000. Information from Jutta Hoschek per email dated November 28, 2014.

5. The company's high expectations for its personnel are illustrated by the fact that in 1912 one of their own in-house "schools" for salesladies was inaugurated. See Pierre Schmiedeknecht, "Im Visier des aufkommenden Nationalsozialismus: Die Entwicklung des Erfurter Kaufhauses Römischer Kaiser von seiner Gründung bis zum Ende der Weimarer Republik" [In the Crosshairs of Rising National Socialism: The Development of the Erfurt Department Store Römischer Kaiser: From Its Founding to the End of the Weimar Republic] (bachelor's thesis, University of Erfurt, 2013), 16–19.

6. For the biography and legacy of Adolf Schmalix, see Steffen Rassloff, *Flucht in die nationale Volksgemeinschaft: Das Erfurter Bürgertum zwischen Kaiserreich and NS-Diktatur* [Escape into National Community: The Erfurt Middle Class between the German Empire and the NS Dictatorship]

(Cologne: Veröffentlichung der Historischen Kommission für Thüringen, 2003), 341–59. See also Steffen Rassloff, "'Erfurt begeht moralischen Selbstmord': Adolf Schmalix und die Grossdeutsche Freiheitsbewegung" ["Erfurt Commits Moral Suicide": Adolf Schmalix and Greater Germany's Freedom Movement], *Stadt und Geschichte: Zeitschrift für Erfurt* 13, no. 4 (2001): 28ff; Steffen Rassloff, *Bürgerkrieg und die Goldene Zwanziger: Erfurt in der Weimarer Republik* [Civil War and the Golden Twenties: Erfurt in the Weimar Republic] (Erfurt, Germany: Sutton Verlag, 2008), 102–7; Monika Kahl, "Adolf Schmalix und die faschistische 'Grossdeutsche Volkspartei'" [Adolf Schmalix and the Fascist "Greater German Folk Party"], *Zeitschrift für Geschichtswissenschaft* 24, no. 5 (1976): 547–58.

7. *Echo Germania* 3, no. 26 (1927).

8. *Echo Germania* 3, no. 42 (1927).

9. See Menzel, *Kaufhaus*, 50–52.

10. Rassloff, "Erfurt begeht moralschen Selbstmord," 28.

11. Hoschek, *Ausgelöschtes Leben*, 10ff.

12. Hoschek, 10ff.

13. Both the city and administrative district of Erfurt were Prussian until 1945; with respect to party politics, they belonged to the Nationalsozialistische Deutsche Arbeiterpartei (NSDAP) Gau Thüringen (National Socialist Administrative District of Thuringia), founded in 1925.

14. Curriculum vitae of Willy Wiemokli; sworn affidavit by Willy Wiemokli for Ernst Wolfgang Topf, December 28, 1945, LaTh–HStAW, Landeskommission zur Durchführung der Befehle (State Commission for Implementation of Orders) 124/126, no. 4651, leaf 99.

"Mischling of the First Degree"

1. Curriculum vitae of Willy Wiemokli.

2. *Vernehmungsprotokoll* (interrogation transcript), January 11, 1943, LaTh–StAG, Amtsgericht Erfurt (Magistrate's Court of Erfurt), no. 1006, *Strafsache* (criminal case) Wyjmoklyj, David, leaf 3.

3. Salomon Adler-Rudel, *Jüdische Selbsthilfe unter dem Naziregime 1933–1939: Im Spiegel der Berichte der Reichsvertretung der Juden in Deutschland* [Jewish Self-Help under the Nazi Regime 1933–1939: Reflected in the

Reports of Reich Representation of Jews in Germany] (Tübingen: Mohr, 1974), 148.

4. Curriculum vitae of Willy Wiemokli.

In Buchenwald

1. Jerzy Tomaszewski and Victoria Pollmann, *Auftakt zur Vernichtung: Die Vertreibung polnischer Juden aus Deutschland im Jahre 1938* [Prelude to Extermination: Expulsion from Germany of Polish Jews in 1938] (Osnabrück: Fibre, 2002), 21.

2. Tomaszewski and Pollman, 90ff.

3. Tomaszewski and Pollman, 106.

4. Hoschek, *Ausgelöschtes Leben*, 13.

5. Juden-Aktion [Jew Action], November 1938, StadtA Erfurt 5/810-7, leaves 1–10. Jutta Hoschek, "Novemberpogrom 1938 in Erfurt: Aus Dokumenten und Erinnerungen" [November Progrom 1938 in Erfurt: In Documents and Memories], in *Landeshauptstadt Erfurt: Stadtverwaltung und Netzwerk "Jüdisches Leben Erfurt"* [Capital City Erfurt: City Administration and Network "Jewish Life Erfurt"] (Jena, Germany: Vopelius Verlag, 2014), 9–11.

6. Curriculum vitae of Willy Wiemokli.

7. In a questionnaire for the committee Victims of Fascism of the city administration of the city of Erfurt, October 26, 1945, 3, LaTh–HStAW, District Assembly and Council of the District of Erfurt—VdN no. 3513, leaf 12r.

8. Hoschek, "Novemberpogrom 1938 in Erfurt," 12–15.

9. Questionnaire "Opfer des Faschismus" [Victim of Fascism].

10. Harry Stein, Gedenkstätte Buchenwald (Buchenwald Memorial), confirmed via email, December 16, 2014, that the arrests of Mischlinge during the November pogrom were the exception, not the rule.

11. The lists under discussion have a cover sheet drawn up in KZ Buchenwald saying "Juden-Aktion November 1938" [Jew Action November 1938] as a copy in the Erfurt City Archive (StadtA Erfurt). Thanks to Harry Stein for his suggestions and help in deciphering and interpreting the documents. Also based on another list drawn up in Buchenwald on November

10, 1938, "of new arrivals delivered from Erfurt" with 188 names we have the number of Erfurt prisoners in Buchenwald at 189. On this list there are eight men who had been arrested in Heiligenstadt and probably had been brought to Buchenwald by way of Erfurt. See Hoschek, "Novemberpogrom 1938 in Erfurt," 58. On the other hand, all the people on the short list of eight names drawn up by Hackmann are not listed among the "new arrivals" except for Heinz Löwenstein, and thus David Wyjmoklyj is also missing. Also missing are Julius Vogel and Hans Schimmelberg, the two men from the list with nine people. These nine Erfurt men must therefore be counted as the "new arrivals," and the eight men from Heiligenstadt do not count as being in the Erfurt arrivals. Cited lists of new arrivals from Erfurt delivered November 10, 1938, ITS, 1.1.5.1/5278099-5278100.

12. Cited list of November 26, 1938, of released Jews from the "Jew Action," November 26, 1938, ITS, 1.1.5.1/5278153.

13. Curriculum vitae of Willy Wiemokli; address books of the city of Erfurt for the years 1931–32 to 1941–42.

14. Address books of the city of Erfurt for the years 1937–38.

At Topf & Söhne

1. Curriculum vitae of Willy Wiemokli.

2. Annegret Schüle, *Industrie und Holocaust: Topf & Söhne—Die Ofenbauer von Auschwitz* [Industry and Holocaust: Topf & Söhne—Builders of the Ovens of Auschwitz], 2nd ed. (Göttingen: Wallstein Verlag, 2011), 107–15.

3. Sales list of Kurt Prüfer, Department D IV, January–March 1941, LaTh–HStAW, J. A. Topf & Söhne no. 14, leaf 111r.

4. Corrected account by Willy Wiemokli for the sales by Kurt Prüfer 1936–41 (First Quarter), August 2, 1941, LaTh–HStAW, J. A. Topf & Söhne no. 15, leaf 107.

5. Schüle, *Industrie und Holocaust*, 134.

Love

1. Curriculum vitae of Erika Wiemokli, January 3, 1984, LaTh–HStAW, J. A. Topf & Söhne no. 15, leaf 26.

2. Questionnaire "Victim of Fascism."
3. Sworn affidavit by Wiemokli for Ernst Wolfgang Topf.
4. Curriculum vitae of Erika Wiemokli.

Father's Deportation and Murder

1. Beate Meyer, *"Jüdische Mischlinge": Rassenpolitik und Verfolgungserfahrung 1933–1945* ["Jewish Mischlinge": Racial Policy and the Experience of Persecution 1933–1945], 3rd ed. (Hamburg: Dölling und Galitz, 2007), 94.

2. After consulting with Hitler at the end of 1938, Hermann Göring set forth, among other topics, the status of Mischehen anew in a secret memorandum. See, for example, guidelines (secret) of those responsible for the four-year plan of December 28, 1938, in Aly Götz et al., eds., *Die Verfolgung und Ermordung der europäischen Juden durch das nationalsozialistische Deutschland 1933–1945* [The Persecution and Murder of the European Jews by National Socialist Germany 1933–1945] (Berlin and Munich: Bundesarchiv [Federal Archive] and Institut für Zeitgeschichte [Institute for Contemporary History], 2011), Document 215, 583ff.

3. Meyer, *"Jüdische Mischlinge,"* 30. See also Ursula Büttner, "Bollwerk Familie: Die Rettung der Juden in 'Mischehen'" [Family as Bulwark: The Salvation of Jews in "Mischehen"], in *Mut zur Menschlichkeit: Hilfe für Verfolgte während der NS-Zeit* [Courage to Humanity: Help for the Persecuted during the NS Era], ed. Günter B. Ginzel (Cologne: Landschaftsverband Rheinland, 1993), 59–77, here 66ff.

4. *Polizeiverordnung über die Kennzeichnung der Juden* [Police Decree on Identification of Jews], September 1, 1941, *Reichsgesetzblatt* [Reich Legal Registry] I (1941) no. 100, 547. The exceptions were set forth in paragraph 3. Accordingly, the identification requirement did not extend to "den in einer Mischehe lebenden jüdischen Ehegatten, sofern Abkömmlinge aus der Ehe vorhanden sind und nicht als Juden gelten [as defined by the Nuremberg Laws, authors], und zwar auch dann, wenn die Ehe nicht mehr besteht . . ." (the Jewish spouse living in a mixed marriage insofar as offspring exist from the marriage and do not count as Jews [as defined by the Nuremberg Laws, authors], and even if the marriage no longer exists . . .).

5. Beate Meyer, "Fragwürdiger Schutz: Mischehen in Hamburg (1933–1945)" [Questionable Protection: Mixed Marriages in Hamburg, 1933–1945], in *Die Verfolgung und Ermordung der Hamburger Juden 1933–1945, Geschichte, Zeugnis, Erinnerung* [The Persecution and Murder of the Jews of Hamburg, History, Witness, Memory], ed. Beate Meyer (Hamburg: Institut für die Geschichte der Deutschen Juden, 2006), 79–88, here 87.

6. Hoschek, *Ausgelöschtes Leben*, 15–17. See also "Deportation und Ermordung der Thüringer Juden 1942–1945" [Deportation and Murder of the Jews of Thuringia 1942–1945], in *Erinnerungsort Topf & Söhne: Die Ofenbauer von Auschwitz Erfurt* [Topf & Söhne: Bulders of the Ovens of Auschwitz Place of Remembrance Erfurt] (Erfurt, Germany: Landeshauptstadt Erfurt, Stadtverwaltung, 2013) 11–15. See also Carsten Liesenberg and Harry Stein, *Deportation und Vernichtung der Thüringer Juden 1942* [Deportation and Destruction of the Jews of Thuringia 1942] (Erfurt, Germany: Quellen zur Geschichte Thüringens 39, Landeszentrale für politische Bildung Thüringen, 2012).

7. Curriculum vitae of Willy Wiemokli.

8. LaTh–StAG, Amtsgericht Erfurt (Magistrate's Court of Erfurt) no. 1006, *Strafsache* (criminal case) Wyjmoklyj, David, leaves 1–5.

9. *Zweite Verordnung zur Durchführung des Gesetzes über die Änderung von Familiennamen und Vornamen* [Second Decree on the Execution of the Law regarding Changing Surnames and Forenames], August 17, 1938, *Reichsgesetzblatt* 1, no. 130 (1938): 1044.

10. City Prison of Erfurt, *Mitteilung des Abganges eines Gefangenen oder Verwahrten* [Notice of a Prisoner or Detainee Departure], April 16, 1943, LaTh–StAG, Amtsgericht Erfurt no. 1006, *Strafsache* (criminal case) Wyjmoklyj, David, leaf 15. Albrecht Loth, LaTh–StAG, confirmed via email on December 18, 2014, that it was the prison on Andreasstrasse.

11. Andreas T. Schneider, *Die Geheime Staatspolizei im NS-Gau Thüringen: Geschichte, Struktur, Personal und Wirkungsfelder* [The Secret State Police in the NS District of Thuringia: History, Structure, Personnel, and Fields of Activity] (Frankfurt: Verlag für Polizeiwissenschaft, 2008), 302–16, regarding the field office Erfurt South, 94–96.

12. Schneider, 158, 333.

13. City Prison of Erfurt.

14. Curriculum vitae Willy Wiemokli.

15. Death certificate of David Wyjmoklyj. See also "Sterbebücher von Auschwitz-Birkenau: Fragmente" [Death Books from Auschwitz-Birkenau], ed. Staatliches Museum Auschwitz-Birkenau: Fragments, 3 (Name Index M–Z) (Munich and Saur: De Gruyter, 1995), 1372. Also see Morgue Book, APMO, D-Aul-5/2, 168. On the responsibility for the crematoria and on the falsification of the cause of death in Auschwitz, see Thomas Grotum, *Das digitale Archiv: Aufbau und Auswertung einer Datenbank zur Geschichte des Konzentrationslagers Auschwitz* [The Digital Archive: Building and Evaluating a Data Bank on the History of the Concentration Camp of Auschwitz] (Frankfurt and New York: Campus, 2004), 228, 297ff. See also Tadeusz Paczula, "Schreibstuben im KL Auschwitz" [Orderlies' Offices in KL Auschwitz], in *Sterbebücher von Auschwitz: Fragmente Bd 1 (Berichte)* [Death Books of Auschwitz: Fragments 1 (Reports)], ed. Staatliches Museum Auschwitz-Birkenau (State Museum Auschwitz-Birkenau) (Munich and London: K. G. Saur, 1995), 27–66. For the work assignments of Friedrich Entress and Maximilian Grabner, see http://www.wollheimmemorial.de/en/selektionen_und_menschenversuche_im_haeftlingskrankenbau. See also Ernst Klee, *Auschwitz: Täter, Gehilfen, Opfer und was aus ihnen wurde: Ein Personenlexikon* [Auschwitz: Perpetrators, Helpers, Victims and What Became of Them: A Biographical Lexicon] (Frankfurt: S. Fischer, 2013), 108ff, 146ff.

16. Hoschek, *Ausgelöschtes Leben*, 488ff.

17. Hoschek, 16ff. Like Willy Wiemokli, Helmut (1925–44) and Rosemarie Cohn (1928–45) were Mischlinge of the first degree. They were caught up in the snares of the Gestapo when neighbors denounced them—they were immediately deported and died in the concentration camps—one in Buchenwald and the other in Bergen-Belsen. See Hoschek, 81–83.

18. Curriculum vitae of Willy Wiemokli.

Forced-Labor Camp

1. Minutes of the Wannsee Conference of January 20, 1942, in *Die Wannsee-Konferenz am 20. Januar 1942: Dokumente, Forschungsstand, Kontroversen* [The Wannsee Conference on January 20, 1942: Documents,

Status of Research, Controversies], ed. Norbert Kampe and Peter Klein (Cologne: Böhlau, 2013), 17–115, here 40–54.

2. Not only did Mischlinge of the first degree have to serve in the military after 1935, but they were even called up at the beginning of the war in 1939; however, in April 1940 they were released from the military by a decree of expulsion. Call-ups to physicals still took place and in the cases where the recruit was found fit to serve, the recruit was assigned to reserve units. Meyer, *"Jüdische Mischlinge,"* 231. Theoretically, Wiemokli could also have been drafted. It isn't known whether he had a *UK-Stellung* (*Unabkömmlichstellung*, or an indispensable job) as other coworkers had, especially including members of the Communist Party. For UK-Stellungen at Topf & Söhne, see Schüle, *Industrie und Holocaust*, 96ff.

3. Wolf Gruner, "Die NS-Führung und Zwangsarbeit für sogenannte jüdische Mischlinge: Ein Einblick in Planung und Praxis antijüdischer Politik in den Jahren 1942–1944" [NS Leadership and Forced Labor for So-Called Jewish Mischlinge 1942–1944], and Wolf Gruner, "Ein Einblick in Planung und Praxis anitjüdischer Politik" [An Examination of Planning and Practice of Anti-Jewish Policies], in *Rassismus, Faschismus, Antifaschismus: Forschungen und Betrachtungen gewidmet Kurt Pätzold zum 70 Geburtstag* [Racism, Fascism, Antifascism: Studies and Considerations Dedicated to Kurt Pätzold on his 70th Birthday], ed. Manfred Weissbecker and Reinhard Kühnl (Cologne: PapyRossa, 2000), 63–79, here 65–71. See also Meyer, *"Jüdische Mischlinge,"* 238. For the numbers of the forced laborers in the Todt Organization, see Franz W. Seidler, *Die Organisation Todt: Bauen für Staat und Wehrmacht 1938–1945* [The Todt Organization: Building for the State and Army 1938–1945] (Koblenz, Germany: Bernard & Graefe, 1987), 140–47.

4. Fritz Sauckel (1894–1946) had been gauleiter in Thuringia since 1927, and had been a member of the NSDAP since 1923. See Steffen Rassloff, *Fritz Sauckel: Hitler's "Muster-Gauleiter" und "Sklavenhalter"* [Fritz Sauckel: Hitler's "Model Gauleiter" and "Slave Master"], 3rd ed. (Erfurt, Germany: Landeszentrale für politische Bildung Thüringen, 2008), 91–103.

5. Gruner, *Zwangsarbeit*, 71–74; Meyer, *"Jüdische Mischlinge,"* 238–47.

6. Curriculum vitae of Willy Wiemokli.

7. Testimony of Willy Wyjmoklyj, defendant in the trial for crimes against Order no. 160 SMAD (Soviet Military Administration in Germany) in the regional court of Erfurt, II, Criminal Senate, February 16, 1953, LaTh–HStAW, Bezirksstaatsanwaltschaft (regional state prosecutor's office) no. 1213, leaf 216r.

8. Sworn statement of Ingeborg Prior, secretary for Ernst Wolfgang Topf, January 3, 1946, Denazification file of Ernst Wolfgang Topf, HStAW, Abt. 520, no. BW 4329 Wiesbaden, leaves 28–32; Sworn statement of Wiemokli for Ernst Wolfgang Topf.

Back at Topf & Söhne

1. Curriculum vitae of Willy Wiemokli.

2. Written report about the discussion, in the files of the shop committee, April 27, 1945, LaTh–HStAW, Collection of Jean-Claude Pressac no. 34, leaves 229ff; Schüle, *Industrie und Holocaust*, 240–45.

3. Schüle, 237–62.

Loyalty

1. Sworn statement of Wiemokli for Ernst Wolfgang Topf.

2. Written report of shop committee meeting on October 29, 1945, LaTh–HStAW, J. A. Topf & Söhne no. 451, leaf 71.

3. Written report of shop committee meeting on February 19, 1946, LaTh–HStAW, J. A. Topf & Söhne no. 451, leaf 46.

4. Schüle, *Industrie und Holocaust*, 267.

At the Head of the Company

1. Schüle, *Industrie und Holocaust*, 268–85, especially 285.

2. Memo to file by Max Machemehl, May 16, 1946, LaTh–HStAW, J. A. Topf & Söhne no. 15, leaf 62.

3. Memo to file by Willy Wiemokli, May 18, 1946, LaTh–HStAW, J. A. Topf & Söhne no. 15, leaf 61.

4. Basis for judgment against Willy Wyjmoklyj, District Court Erfurt II, Criminal Division, November 18, 1953, LaTh–HStAW, District State Prosecutor's Office Erfurt no. 1213, leaf 61.

5. Testimony of defendant Willy Wyjmoklyj, leaf 216v.

6. Schüle, *Industrie und Holocaust*, 281–93. NAGEMA is the acronym for *Nährung* (NA, food), *Genussmittel* (GE, alcohol and tobacco), and *Maschinenbau* (MA, mechanical engineering).

Designation as a Persecuted Person of the Nazi Regime

1. "Richtlinien für die Anerkennung als Verfolgte des Naziregimes des Ministeriums für Arbeits- und Gesundheitswesen der DDR" [Guidelines for Certification as Persecuted Persons of the Nazi Regime of the Ministry of Labor and Health of the GDR], February 18, 1950, *Gesetzblatt der Deutschen Demokratischen Republik* [Law Gazette of the German Democratic Republic] 1, no. 14 (1950): 92–94.

2. Questionnaire *Opfer des Faschismus*; Sworn affidavit by Wiemokli for Ernst Wolfgang Topf.

3. *Beschluss des Prüfungsausschusses beim Kreisratsamt/Rat der Stadt, Sozialamt, Referat VdN (VdN Kreisdienststelle)*, November 14, 1951 [Decision of the Review Committee of the District Office/City Council, Social Welfare Office, VdN department for VdN District Office], LaTh–HStAW, District Council and Erfurt District Council, VdN no. 3513, leaf 7.

4. Schüle, *Industrie und Holocaust*, 313.

Investigation of Company Management

1. Testimony of defendant Willy Wyjmoklyj, leaf 216v.

2. Schüle, *Industrie und Holocaust*, 318–22.

3. Testimony of defendant Willy Wyjmoklyj, leaf 216v.

4. Nikos Belojannis (also spelled Belogiannis or Beloyannis) was a Greek Communist who had been imprisoned in a German concentration camp in Greece and executed in 1952 in his native country. See Schüle, *Industrie und Holocaust*, 298–300.

Imprisonment Again for Wiemokli

1. Testimony of defendant Willy Wyjmoklyj. Judgment against Willy Wyjmoklyj, District Court Erfurt II, Criminal Division, November 18, 1953, LaTh–HStAW, District State Prosecutor's Office Erfurt no. 1213, leaves 59–80; *Das Volk*, February 27, 1953.

2. Judgment against Willy Wyjmoklyj, leaf 79.

3. Letter from the attorney Reuter to the District Court II Criminal Division, February 10, 1953, LaTh–HStAW, District State Prosecutor's Office Erfurt no. 1213, leaves 197ff.

4. Resolution of the SED company's party organization in the Machine Works Nikos Belojannis, February 13, 1953, LaTh–HStAW, District State Prosecutor's Office Erfurt no. 1213/3, leaf 38.

5. Basis for judgment against Willy Wyjmoklyj.

6. Sentence of Willy Wyjmoklyj, leaves 79ff.

7. Sentence of Willy Wyjmoklyj, leaf 59.

8. Decision of the review committee of the District Council/City Council, Social Welfare Office, Report VdN (VdN-Regional Office), March 5, 1953, LaTh–HStAW, District Assembly and Council of the District of Erfurt—VdN no. 3513, leaf 4.

Rehabilitation

1. Letter from the VdN office to the District State Prosecutor's Office, August 5, 1953, LaTh–HStAW, District State Prosecutor's Office no. 1213, leaf 7.

2. Petition for clemency from Erika Wyjmoklyj, July 18, 1953; Letter from residents of Willy Wyjmoklyj's apartment house to State Prosecutor Klapp, July 22, 1953, LaTh–HStAW, District State Prosecutor's Office Erfurt no. 1213/2, leaves 1 and 5.

3. VdN Identity Card of Willi Wiemokli, LaTh–HStAW, District Assembly and Council of the District of Erfurt—VdN no. 3513, leaves 22a–23b.

4. Letter from Willy Wiemokli to the Erfurt City Senate, Social Welfare Office, Report VdN, August 5, 1957, LaTh–HStAW, District Assembly and Council of the District of Erfurt–VdN no. 3513, leaf 21r.

5. Petition for clemency by Erika Wyjmoklyj.

6. Curriculum vitae of Erika Wiemokli.

7. People's Police District Office Erfurt, Report of Conduct for Willy Wyjmoklyj, March 15, 1956, LaTh–HStAW, District State Prosecutor's Office Erfurt no. 1213, leaf 22.

8. Petition for clemency by Erika Wyjmoklyj.

9. Letter from Willy Wiemokli to the District VdN Commission of Erfurt, March 10, 1975, LaTh–HStAW, District Assembly and Council for the District of Erfurt—VdN no. 3513, leaf 32r.

10. Questionnaire for application to qualify as a VdN surviving dependent, January 3, 1984, Decision of the VdN Regional Commission Erfurt, January 11, 1984, LaTh–HStAW, District Assembly and Council of the District of Erfurt—VdN no. 3513, leaf 25, 27r.

Concluding Comments

1. Arnold Zweig, "Halbjuden" [Half Jews], in *Die Sammlung: Literarische Monatsschrift unter dem Patronat von André Gide, Aldous Huxley, Heinrich Mann* [The Collection: Literary Monthly under the Patronage of André Gide, Aldous Huxley, Heinrich Mann], ed. Klaus Mann (Munich: Verlag Rogner und Bernhard/Zweitausendeins, 1987), 287–90, here 287.

2. Curriculum vitae of Willy Wiemokli.

3. Schüle, *Industrie und Holocaust*, 89.

4. Meyer, *"Jüdische Mischlinge,"* 373.

5. Meyer, 382.

Translator's Afterword

1. "This man, a certain Müller, a blond man . . . is a Jew, a star-wearing Jew, but before his Jewishness was ascertained he was an SA member, is still friends with his former comrades, . . . and is said to have Gestapo permission to conceal his star on the street." See Victor Klemperer, *I Will Bear Witness: A Diary of the Nazi Years 1942–1933*, trans. Martin Chalmers (New York: Random House, 1998), 262.

2. "What we need is not to be told yet again the facts about mass murder, but to understand why it took place and how people could carry it out." See Richard J. Evans, *The Third Reich in History and Memory* (New York: Oxford Univ. Press, 2015), 398.

3. Leopold von Ranke, "Preface to the First Edition [1824]," in *Geschichten der romanischen und germanischen Völker von 1494 bis 1514* [History of the Latin and Teutonic Nations from 1494 to 1514], 3rd ed. (Leipzig: Verlag von Dunder & Humblot, 1885), https://archive.org/details/geschich tenderro00rankuoft.

4. The Holocaust denier David Irving sued the historian Deborah Lipstadt for libel after Penguin published *Denying the Holocaust: The Growing Assault on Truth and Memory* (1993). Under British law, the burden of proof lies with the defendant. In this trial, no eyewitnesses were called; the defense successfully relied on massive historical scholarship. The *Daily Telegraph* commented on the significance of the verdict: "The Irving case has done for the new century what the Nuremberg tribunals or the Eichmann trial did for earlier generations"—see http://www.hdot.org/en/trial/. One of the defense expert witnesses, Robert Jan van Pelt, wrote a seven-hundred-page report on the historical evidence for the gas chambers and ovens. In his introduction to *The Case for Auschwitz: Evidence from the Irving Trial* (Bloomington: Indiana Univ. Press, 2002), van Pelt writes, "the so-called question of the gas chambers has become a pivot of Holocaust denial, or negationism, as I will call it," ix.

5. Martin Gilbert, *The Holocaust: A History of the Jews of Europe during the Second World War* (New York: Holt, Rinehart, and Winston, 1985), 46.

6. Evans, *The Third Reich in History and Memory*, 40.

7. Monika Gibas, ed., *Fates of Jewish Families in Thuringia 1933–1945*, trans. Julia Palme (Erfurt, Germany: Landeszentrale für politische Bildung Thüringen, 2009), 7.

8. Gibas, 8.

9. Harry Stein, *Konzentrationslager Buchenwald 1937–1945: Begleitband zur ständigen historischen Ausstellung* [Concentration Camp Buchenwald 1937–1945: Volume Accompanying the Permanent History Exhibit], ed. Gedenkstätte Buchenwald (Buchenwald Memorial) (Göttingen: Wallenstein Verlag, 1999), 111–15.

10. Klemperer, *I Will Bear Witness*, December 11, 1944, 382.

11. Klemperer, May 30, 1942, 63.

12. Klemperer, June 27, 1942, 87.

13. Klemperer, March 27, 1942, 34.

14. Klemperer, May 3, 1942, 47.

15. Klemperer, May 11, 1942, 51.

16. "Als nicht arisch gilt, wer von nicht arischen, insbesondere jüdischen Eltern oder Grosseltern abstammt. Es genügt, wenn ein Elternteil oder ein Grosselternteil nicht arisch ist. . . . Wer als Reichsbeamter berufen werden soll, hat nachzuweisen, dass er und seine Ehegatte arischer Abstammung sind. Jeder Reichsbeamte, der eine Ehe eingehen will, hat nachzuweisen, dass die Person, mit der er die Ehe eingehen will, arischer Abstammung ist." *Reichsgesetzblatt* [Reich Legal Gazette], 1933, 575. Guidelines to § 1 a Abs. 3 of the *Reichsbeamtengesetz* (Civil Service Restoration Act) in the version of the law of June 30, 1933 (issued August 8, 1933), documentArchiv.de, http://www.documentArchiv.de/ns/rbeamtenges-1a_rtl.html.

17. § 6.2: "Sonstige Anforderung an die Reinheit des Blutes, die über § 5 hinausgehen, dürfen nur mit Zustimmung des Reichsministers des Innern und des Stellvertreters des Führers gestellt werden. . . ." § 7: "Der Führer und Reichskanzler kann Befreiung von den Vorschriften der Ausführungsverordnungen erteilen." The English version of this law and other documents can be found in Jeremy Noakes and Geoffrey Pridham, eds., *Documents on Nazism, 1919–1945* (New York: Viking, 1974).

18. "Runderlass des Reichs—und Preussischen Ministers des Innern vom 26: November 1935 über das 'Verbot von Rassenmischen,'" *Ministerialblatt für die Preussische Innere Verwaltung* 49 (1935): 1429–34; cited in Michael Burleigh and Wolfgang Wippermann, *The Racial State: Germany 1933–1945* (Cambridge: Cambridge Univ. Press, 1991), 332. See also Cornelia Schmitz-Berning, *Vokabular des Nationalsozialismus* [The Vocabulary of National Socialism] (Berlin and New York: Walter de Gryter, 1998), 408–10.

19. Richard J. Evans, "Nazi Policy towards 'Half-Jews' and 'Mixed Marriages,'" *David Irving: Hitler and Holocaust Denial*, Holocaust Denial on Trial, Emory University, https://www.hdot.org/evans/#.

20. "Repealing of Nazi Laws," Allied Control Council's Law no. 1 (CCL 1), signed by L. Koeltz (France), B. L. Montgomery (Great Britain), V. D.

Sokolovsky (Soviet Union), and Dwight D. Eisenhower (United States), https://www.loc.gov/rr/frd/Military_Law/Enactments/Volume-I.pdf.

21. Bruno Blau, "The Jewish Population of Germany, 1939–1945," *Jewish Social Studies* 12, no. 2 (April 1950): 161–72.

22. Blau, 166. "Mosaic" indicated adherence to the Jewish religion. The person was registered as a member of the Jewish community.

23. United States Holocaust Memorial Museum, "German Jewish Refugees, 1933–1939," https://www.ushmm.org/wlc/en/article.php?Module Id=10005468.

24. Blau, "The Jewish Population of Germany," 171. United States Holocaust Memorial Museum, "German Refugees, 1933–1939," states that there were approximately 202,000 Jews in Germany at the end of 1939.

25. East Germany Synagogues, "Erfurt–Thuringia," http://www.east germanysynagogues.com/index.php/communities/101-erfurt-thuringia -english.

26. Yad Vashem, "Erfurt, Provinz Sachsen, Deutsches Reich," http:// db.yadvashem.org/deportation/place.html?language=de&itemId=5428439.

27. Jewish Virtual Library, https://www.jewishvirtuallibrary.org/erfurt.

28. Philippe Sands, *East West Street: On the Origins of "Genocide" and "Crimes Against Humanity"* (New York: Knopf, 2016), 103, citing the case decided in 1940 by the Reich Supreme Court, which H. Lauterpacht described in the *Annual Digest and Reports of Public International Law Cases*, vol. 9 (London: Butterworth & Co. 1942).

29. Nicholas Stargardt, *The German War: A Nation under Arms, 1939–1945* (New York: Basic Books, 2015), 88. See also, "'Anyone who continues to uphold personal contacts with him [the Jew],' Goebbels wrote in his article in *Das Reich* on 16 November [1941], 'is taking his side and must be treated as a Jew,'" 242.

30. Rachel E. Boaz, "The Search for 'Aryan Blood': Seroanthropology in Weimar and National Socialist Germany" (PhD diss., Kent State University, 2009), 253–54.

31. Meyer, "*Jüdische Mischlinge*," 126.

32. Meyer, 127.

33. Thomas Pegelow, "Determining 'People of German Blood,' 'Jews' and 'Mischlinge': The Reich Kinship Office and the Competing Discourses

and Powers of Nazism, 1941–1943," *Contemporary European History* 15, no. 1 (February 2006): 50.

34. Pegelow, 52.

35. Meyer, "*Jüdische Mischlinge*," 113.

36. Meyer, 111.

37. Laureen Nussbaum, "Shedding Our Stars: How German Lawyer Hans Calmeyer Saved Thousands of Jewish Lives in Occupied Holland (1941–1944)" (unpublished manuscript). See also "Calmeyer, Hans (1903–1972)," http://db.yadvashem.org/righteous/family.html?language=en&itemId=4042996.

38. Victor Klemperer, *The Lesser Evil: The Diaries of Victor Klemperer 1945–59*, trans. Martin Chalmers (London: Phoenix, 2004), 70: "We still need 3 attestations that we wore the star," and 195: "I had helped them get an attestation that Bernhard had worn the Jew's star. The Americans had not believed them . . ."

39. *Merriam-Webster's Collegiate Dictionary* defines a regenerative furnace as a gas-burning furnace with a regenerator; namely, "a chamber filled with checkerwork that is repeatedly heated by exhaust gases in order to heat air that is passed through it."

40. Anonymous, "Progress of Cremation," *British Medical Journal* 1, no. 2566 (March 1910): 581.

41. Simone Ameskamp, "On Fire: Cremation in Germany, 1870s–1934" (PhD diss., Georgetown University, 2006), 3.

42. Ameskamp, 11.

43. Topf & Söhne, "A Perfectly Normal Company: The Cremation Act of 1934," http://topfundsoehne.info/cms-www/index.php?id=97&l=1.

44. Schüle, *Industrie und Holocaust*.

45. Schüle, 9.

46. "[Alfred Toepfer] acted in the same way as many other businessmen in the Third Reich: he worked to win powerful patrons within the Nazi regime, securing, for example, the good offices of Hermann Göring, and appointing top SS men to senior positions in his Foundation." See Evans, *The Third Reich in History and Memory*, 216. Evans also refers to Martin Broszat's *The Hitler State* (1981), which uncovered "the true breadth and

depth of complicity of German social, economic and political elites in the rise, triumph and rule of the Nazis" (235).

47. Schüle, *Industrie und Holocaust*, 85.

48. Schüle, 108–9.

49. Schüle, 113.

50. Schüle, 125.

51. Annegret Schüle, *J. A. Topf & Söhne: Ein Erfurter Familienunternehmen und der Holocaust* [J. A. Topf & Söhne: An Erfurt Family Company and the Holocaust] (Erfurt, Germany: Landeszentral für politische Bildung Thüringen, 2014), 63–65.

52. Schüle, *Industrie und Holocaust*, 464; Schüle, *Ein Erfurter Familienunternehmen*, 79.

53. Schüle, *Industrie und Holocaust*, 327–30.

54. Schüle, 328–29.

55. Eli M. Rosenbaum, "German Company Got Crematorium Patent," *New York Times*, July 27, 1993; response to "Engineers of Death," Op-Ed by Gerald Fleming, *New York Times*, July 18, 1993.

56. Patrick Greaney, "Last Words: Expression and Quotation in the Works of Luis Camnitzer," *Germanic Review* 89 (2014): 94–120.

57. Schüle, *Industrie und Holocaust*, 209.

58. Angelika Reiser-Fischer, "Die zwielichtige Ehrung des Heinrich Messing" [The Ambiguous Tribute to Heinrich Messing], *Thüringer Allgemeine*, March 7, 2013.

59. Annika Van Baar and Wim Huisman, "The Oven Builders of the Holocaust: A Case Study of Corporate Complicity in International Crimes," *British Journal of Criminology: An International Review of Crime and Society* 52 (2012): 1033–50.

60. Schüle, *Industrie und Holocaust*, 119.

61. Schüle, 446.

62. Van Baar and Huisman, "The Oven Builders of the Holocaust," 1043.

63. Van Baar and Huisman, 1045.

64. "Zur Person: Günter Gaus im Gespräch mit Hannah Arendt" [Profile: Günter Gaus in Conversation with Hannah Arendt], Rundfunk

Berlin-Brandenburg, October 28, 1964. "Das war wirklich, als ob der Abgrund sich öffnet. Weil man die Vorstellung gehabt hat, alles andere hätte irgendwie noch einmal gutgemacht werden können, . . . Dies nicht. Dies hätte nicht geschehen dürfen. Und damit meine ich nicht die Zahl der Opfer. Ich meine die Fabrikation der Leichen." (It was really as if the abyss opened. Because one had thought that everything else could somehow be made good again, . . . But not this. This should not have been allowed to happen. And by that I don't mean the number of victims. I mean the fabrication of corpses.")

65. Van Baar and Huisman, "The Oven Builders of the Holocaust," 1047.

66. Jeffrey Herf, *Divided Memory: The Nazi Past in the Two Germanys* (Cambridge, MA: Harvard Univ. Press, 1997), 70.

67. Herf, 424n3. The number of Jews in Germany immediately after the war varies with the source. Robin Ostow states the number of Jews who survived to be fifteen thousand in "From the Cold War through the Wende: History, Belonging, and the Self in East German Jewry," *Oral History Review* 21, no. 2 (Winter 1993): 59.

68. Edna Brocke, "Jews in the New Germany: What Has Changed?" *European Judaism: A Journal for the New Europe* 27, no. 2 (Autumn 94): 73.

69. Herf, *Divided Memory*, 71.

70. Herf, 3, 11.

71. Herf, 201ff. Herf's chapter forms the basis of this paragraph on the three possible responses to the Nazi regime, its crimes, and the Holocaust.

72. Herf, 69ff.

73. Herf, 127.

74. Robin Ostow, "From the Cold War through the Wende," 60.

75. Herf, *Divided Memory*, 87.

76. Herf, 94.

77. Herf, 95.

78. Jonathan Kandell, "Imre Kertész, Nobel Laureate Who Survived Holocaust, Dies at 86," *New York Times*, March 31, 2016, quoting a 2001 interview with Kertész by the Spanish newspaper *El País*.

Dr. Annegret Schüle is the curator of the memorial Topf & Sons—Builders of the Auschwitz Ovens Place of Remembrance, which is housed on the former grounds of the firm J. A. Topf & Söhne. She is the acting director of the history museums of the state capital of Erfurt and a private lecturer in modern and contemporary history at the University of Erfurt. Born in Neckarsulm, Germany, in 1959, since 2002 she has been researching the history of a company whose name is synonymous with the ovens of the concentration camps. She has published monographs, articles, and books on the topic.

Tobias Sowade studied history and ethics. He wrote his master's thesis on Willy Wiemokli. Born in Zschopau, Germany, in 1988, he was a research assistant at the University of Erfurt from 2014 to 2017 on topics relating to the period 1933–45. He now teaches in Saxony.

Penny Milbouer has translated Michael Wieck's *A Childhood under Hitler and Stalin: Memoirs of a "Certified" Jew*, Maria Roselli's *The Asbestos Lie: The Past and Present of an Industrial Catastrophe*, and Sammy Gronemann's *Utter Chaos*.